# BRITTANY

# PHILIP'S TRAVEL GUIDES

# BRITTANY

KEITH SPENCE

PHOTOGRAPHY BY JOE CORNISH

GEORGE
PHILIP

*To Penny, who travelled with me*

**OPPOSITE TITLE PAGE** *A cottage sandwiched between giant rocks, near the Pointe du Château, north of Tréguier in the Côtes-d'Armor.*

British Library Cataloguing in Publication Data

Spence, Keith
  Brittany.
  I. Title
  914.4104839

ISBN 0–540–01256–4

Text © Keith Spence 1992
Photographs © Joe Cornish 1992
Maps © George Philip 1992

First published by George Philip Limited,
59 Grosvenor Street, London W1X 9DA

Printed in Hong Kong

# Contents

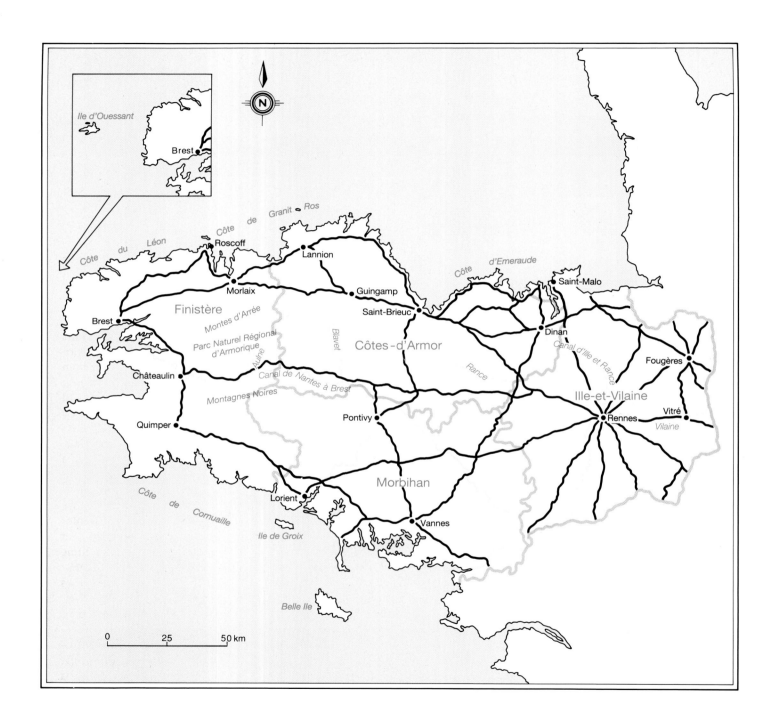

Île d'Ouessant

Brest

N

Côte de Granit Ros

Côte du Léon

Roscoff

Lannion

Morlaix

Finistère

Guingamp

Côte d'Emeraude

Saint-Malo

Montes d'Arrée

Saint-Brieuc

Brest

Parc Naturel Régional d'Armorique

Blavet

Côtes-d'Armor

Dinan

Canal d'Ille et Rance

Fougères

Aulne

Montagnes Noires

Châteaulin

Canal de Nantes à Brest

Rance

Ille-et-Vilaine

Quimper

Pontivy

Rennes

Vitré

Vilaine

Morbihan

Côte de Cornuaille

Lorient

Vannes

Île de Groix

Belle Île

0    25    50 km

# Introduction

Seen on the map, the outline of Brittany is like a battered gargoyle jutting into the Atlantic from the western edge of mainland Europe. About the size of Denmark, with a population of some 3,500,000, Brittany is part of France but, for both geographical and historical reasons, does not feel itself fully to belong to France. Its deeply indented coast, 1200 kilometres long, is cut into hundreds of creeks and small inlets, where towering cliffs alternate with sandy coves or strange moonscapes of splintered rock. Inland, Brittany's 'mountains' seldom exceed 300m in height, yet they can be as rugged and wild as hills three times as high. Their small dimensions belie their immense age: they are all that is left of the Armorican Massif, heaved up from the sea-bed in a geological cataclysm about 500 million years ago, and are thus ten times the age of the Alps. In Brittany granite is never far from the surface, as inland farmers have found to their cost since agriculture was first practised there; though builders and sculptors from the Stone Age to the present day have learned how to master this hardest of all rock and use it to their advantage.

Like Wales, Ireland, Galicia and the other countries of the 'Celtic Fringe', Brittany has had a unique history, distinct from that of the rest of France. This has led to differences that cut across every aspect of life. Down the centuries the Bretons evolved their own religious architecture and celebrations, their own folk festivals, dances and music, their own furniture and costumes, their own food and drink. Above all, they kept their own language, akin to Welsh though now spoken by a smaller proportion of the population; patriotic Bretons still cling to it passionately as a symbol of their national, non-French identity.

For tens of thousands of years Brittany was inhabited by wandering tribes of hunter-gatherers, whose flint tools and weapons can be seen in the archaeological museums at Vannes, Carnac and elsewhere. But the first substantial remains of prehistoric man come from a far later, settled epoch, beginning around the fifth millennium BC – the hundreds of standing stones and burial chambers scattered across the country, which may be isolated in open fields, half-buried in woodland, or engulfed in modern housing.

Brittany makes its first appearance in known European history in about the sixth century BC, when the Gauls arrived in the Breton peninsula, speaking a language not far removed from the Breton of today,

and calling the coast and hinterland of their new country respectively Armor, 'the sea', and Argoat, 'the forest'. Like the rest of Gaul, Brittany was conquered in 56 BC by Julius Caesar, and became the Roman province of Gallia Armorica, 'Gaul by the sea'. As far as the Romans were concerned, Brittany was a remote and impoverished province, and few traces remain of their four centuries of occupation. As Rome's power gradually declined from the third century on, Brittany suffered increasing numbers of attacks by barbarian sea-raiders from the north and east, and relapsed into a state of near-chaos.

During this period of turmoil the first Christian missionaries arrived in the country, along with Celtic refugees from Wales and Cornwall, driven out by invading Angles and Saxons, and bringing with them the Roman name 'Britannia', evolving into 'Bretagne', after the country they had left behind. They ousted the established Druid priesthood, and brought with them their own Celtic church organization, which was a loose federation of monastic settlements, quite different from the rigid territorial divisions of the Roman Catholic church. Virtually every religious leader, however minor, was later revered as a saint, and Brittany has literally thousands of them, mostly unknown elsewhere in Europe. Many Breton place names date from this period: those with Lan- or Lam- as their first syllable were originally monastic settlements, while the prefix Plou- means 'parish'. Along with the legendary miracles of the saints go the even more legendary deeds of King Arthur and his knights, who are claimed by Brittany as well as by Britain.

For several centuries Brittany was ruled by a succession of squabbling warlords, emerging from the Dark Ages in the ninth century. In 845 a Breton nobleman, Nominoë, defeated the Frankish army of Charles II the Bald and made Brittany an independent

*Graceful flying buttresses soar inside the church of Notre Dame de Bon Secours, in the heart of the historic town of Guingamp.*

*Battered by the Atlantic waves, the rocky Côte Sauvage on the western side of the Quiberon peninsula is a violent contrast to the safe, sandy beaches on the sheltered eastern shore.*

kingdom. The monarchy lasted for less than a century, brought to an end by Norman invasions in the early tenth century. Then, in 937, Alain Barbe-Torte ('Alan of the Curly Beard'), grandson of the last Breton king, defeated the Normans and established the duchy of Brittany, which lasted almost 600 years.

During the period of the duchy, Brittany played an important role among the warring states of Western Europe. Though the dukes of Brittany wielded nothing like the power of the neighbouring rulers of France and England, the most successful of them played one side off against another with political shrewdness and diplomatic skill. At this time Brittany reached the height of its cultural and architectural splendour, with castles like the ducal château at Nantes and the frontier fortresses of Fougères and Vitré, the cathedrals at

Quimper and Vannes, and the earliest of Finistère's parish closes – elaborate ecclesiastical building complexes found nowhere else in Europe.

The golden age of the duchy came to an end in 1488, when the reigning duke, François II, made the mistake of engaging in a full-scale battle with the French army at Saint-Aubin-du-Cormier, and was overwhelmingly defeated. François died soon afterwards, leaving the duchy to his 11-year-old daughter Anne – the famous Duchess Anne, commemorated in street and restaurant names all over Brittany. Besides being the last ruler of an independent Brittany, Anne married two French kings, Charles VIII and Louis XII; but she left no son to carry on the ducal line. Her daughter, Claude, married the French king François I, and in 1532 the Breton parliament ceded the duchy's autonomy to France.

All the same, Brittany kept a certain amount of self-determination right up to the French Revolution. It had its own parliament, the Etats, which met periodically until 1788 to decide on local administrative matters. Though the Bretons looked back nostalgically to the days of an independent duchy, they settled down, more or less, under France's centralizing control, apart from an anti-taxation rebellion in 1675, the so-called 'Révolte du Papier Timbré ', under Louis XIV. During the French Revolution the Bretons were mainly royalist, and in the 1790s many of them joined the Chouans – anti-revolutionary forces, allied with the English. Their short-lived opposition ended with their defeat at Quiberon in 1795.

After the Revolution, Brittany, along with the rest of France, was reorganized into today's *départements*. Throughout the nineteenth century it stagnated, as just another poor agricultural province on the outer perimeter of France. In the interests of standardization, the Breton language was discouraged in schools, though its flickering flame was kept alive by a few ardent enthusiasts. Brittany's popularity as a holiday destination, mainly for tourists from Britain, began around 1850, with the establishment of Dinard and other resorts on the northern Côte d'Emeraude, and grew steadily as artists such as Gauguin discovered the unsophisticated appeal of its countryside and people.

During World War I 250,000 Bretons were killed – an enormous loss of life for so small a country; and during World War II Breton Resistance fighters were some of the most dedicated and effective in the whole of France. Relics of the war can be found all round the coast, in the form of massive gun emplacements and defence works built by German-controlled slave labour. Some of the smaller coastal blockhouses have been converted into virtually indestructible seaside homes – a practical, typically French way of turning swords into ploughshares. Towards the end of the war a number of Breton towns, notably Brest, Lorient and Saint-Malo, suffered enormous damage, as the Germans fought savage rearguard actions against the British and American armies of liberation.

The latter part of the twentieth century has seen a dramatic upsurge in every aspect of Breton life. There has been an agricultural revival, concentrated in the north-west round the port of Roscoff; while industrial firms have been encouraged to move to Rennes and other major centres. The streets of towns large and small have been pedestrianized, old country roads have been upgraded and new motorways built, and the countryside is dotted with new houses, less conspicuous than they might otherwise be because built in the traditional Breton way, with white-painted walls and slate roofs. Marinas are opening up all round the coast; while Brittany Ferries, who carry thousands of British holidaymakers each year on their Portsmouth-Saint-Malo and Plymouth-Roscoff routes, are constantly adding to their car-ferry fleet. The new TGV high-speed trains have cut the journey from Paris to Rennes down to three hours, which has serious implications for what is left of Brittany's unspoilt coast and countryside, since it has now become a contender for the attentions of the weekend commuter.

*A peaceful riverside scene in Pont-Aven, where Gauguin and many other artists came to paint in the 1880s and '90s. The little town is still an artistic centre.*

*A set of scales carved in the granite keystone of a window in Rochefort-en-Terre indicates a house built for a merchant.*

There has also been a renaissance in all aspects of popular culture, especially music and dance, and a growth in museums concentrating on regional everyday life. Major annual celebrations, held each summer at Rennes, Quimper and Lorient, bring together musicians and dancers not just from Brittany but from all over the Celtic world, and are showcases for traditional music on bagpipes and other instruments, for thousands of dancers in traditional costume, and for all sorts of fringe events such as jazz concerts and plays. The Breton language is not in such a healthy condition, as it is spoken by only about one-fifth of the population, and the number is said to be steadily declining. Nevertheless, as with Welsh and other minority languages, it is kept alive by young enthusiasts in the universities and outside, at Brest, Lorient and other centres of Breton nationalism; and most road-signs give place names in both the Breton and French forms.

As originally established after the Revolution, Brittany consisted of five *départements*: Ille-et-Vilaine, Côtes-du-Nord, Finistère, Morbihan and Loire-Atlantique. In a local-government reshuffle in the 1960s, Brittany was shorn of Loire-Atlantique, and thus of its ancient capital, Nantes, for centuries the chief city of the duchy. Loire-Atlantique is now part of the Pays de la Loire, which may have a certain geographical logic, but is unacceptable to historically-minded Bretons. The most recent and, it is to be hoped, the last of these changes is the alteration of the name Côtes-du-Nord to Côtes-d'Armor, resuscitating an echo of Brittany's remote Gaulish past.

Though Nantes in particular is well worth a visit, I have included only the four *départements* that constitute today's official Brittany. In any case, Nantes and Loire-Atlantique in general are well covered in James Bentley's *The Loire* in this series.

The six circular routes into which the book is divided begin at towns which have great historical interest, but are not necessarily the principal towns of the regions. Thus the circuits that include the *départemental* capitals of Saint-Brieuc and Rennes begin at Guingamp and Vitré respectively, Guingamp largely because of its convenient position at the hub of a wheel of radiating roads, and Vitré because of its great historical interest, not to mention the friendliness and help I found there. Of the other centres, Saint-Malo has been for centuries the main gateway to Brittany for anyone arriving by sea, Morlaix is a riverside town that combines accessibility with fascinating buildings, while Quimper and Vannes have the dignity of their status as local capitals to add to their interest as fine old towns full of museums and art galleries, and centres of Breton life and traditions. Inevitably, there are large unexplored holes in the centres of the circuits; but the riches of Brittany are so inexhaustible that any detour from the prescribed track is bound to lead you to make your own discoveries, whether of a cluster of standing stones in a lonely field, a grey chapel where painted medieval statues glow in the dark interior, a village square full of flowers, or a harbour restaurant with a view of lobster-pots on the quayside, fishing-boats at anchor and seagulls screaming overhead.

## Further reading

The long-established Michelin *Green Guide*, regularly updated, is an invaluable A-Z gazetteer, with maps of all the major towns and a good many of the smaller ones. It contains useful short introductions to Breton history, art and culture.

*Détours Bretagne*, produced by the Comité Régional de Tourisme in Rennes and revised annually, gives up-to-the-minute details of art galleries, châteaux, festivals etc., complete with addresses, phone numbers and dates and times of opening. The *Guide Pratique*, another annual produced in Rennes, is aimed at tour organizers but contains a vast amount of general information for the tourist. (Both are available from the Rennes Tourist Office, 3 rue d'Espagne, B.P. 4175, 35041 Rennes CEDEX).

A comprehensive series of several dozen colour-illustrated booklets, produced down the years by Jos Le Doaré or Ouest-France, covers every subject under the Breton sun, including legends of towns engulfed by the sea, church organs, and the history of Breton Christian names.

Other useful sources of reference may need to be hunted for in French bookshops. Michel Rénouard's *Nouveau Guide de Bretagne* (also in English), published by Ouest-France, is a gazetteer, illustrated in colour, with hundreds of entries down to the smallest villages. The three paperbacks that make up the *Guide de la Bretagne Mystérieuse* (Presses Pocket) give you all you need to know about legends, saints and any other general oddities.

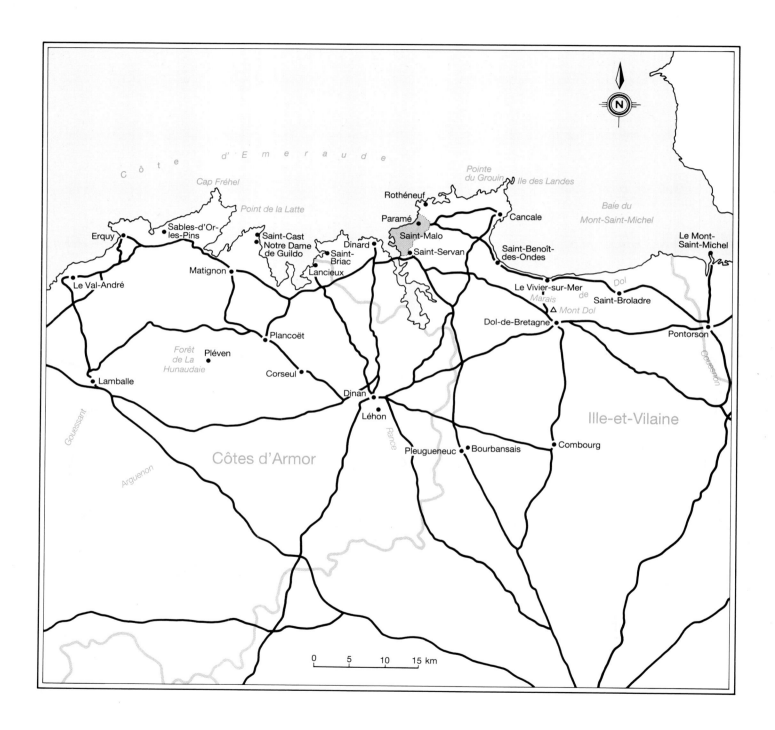

# 1
# The Côte d'Emeraude

*Saint-Malo — Dol-de-Bretagne — Combourg — Dinan*
*Lamballe — Cap Fréhel — Dinard*

For centuries the grey harbour town of Saint-Malo, crouching low at the mouth of the River Rance, was the traveller's first sight of Brittany. Even today, when road access is so easy, the only proper way to approach it is by sea, preferably in the early morning. As the ferry noses slowly past a protecting fringe of rocky islets, the town's massive ramparts, crowned by the needle spire of the cathedral, gradually take shape through the mist. The ship swings round and backs gently into the harbour; and the whole of Brittany lies before you.

The story of Saint-Malo begins not on the present site but on the tiny peninsula of Aleth, which forms the southern arm of the harbour. Under the Roman empire Aleth developed into the capital of a Gaulish tribe, the Curiosolites. In the sixth century a missionary monk from Wales, St Malo — also known as Maclou or Maclaw — landed on Aleth to convert them to Christianity and established a bishopric there. During later centuries constant attacks by raiding Norsemen forced the inhabitants to leave Aleth and take refuge on an uninhabited and more defensible island — the present Saint-Malo, which only became attached to the mainland in the eighteenth century by a steady build-up of sand, known as the Sillon (furrow or causeway).

During the constant wars with the English which bedevilled Brittany throughout the Middle Ages and later, Saint-Malo's geographical position was of great strategic importance, as it guarded the approach up the Rance to the heartland of Brittany. The Malouins, as Saint-Malo people are called, became some of the most skilled sailors in the whole of France, producing generations of corsairs who harried the world's merchant fleets for two centuries or more. During the seventeenth century Saint-Malo was the leading port of France, trading all over the world; and though after 1700 it lost something of its prominence, it remains an important harbour, with dock warehouses and timber yards lining the quays of the inner harbour.

What is astonishing about Saint-Malo is that, for all its air of granite antiquity, almost the whole town was flattened by American bombardment in August 1944 and rebuilt in the post-war years. Fortunately the splendid town wall, with its wide walkway and fortified gateways, survived almost unscathed; to walk the complete circuit only takes about half an hour, and is by far the best way to gain a first impression of the town.

Climb one of the great gates on the harbour side (the Porte Saint-Vincent or the Grande Porte) and head round the walls in a clockwise direction. The rampart walkway is level with the upper windows of the tall grey houses with their steeply pitched roofs, built originally for the *armateurs* (shipowners), who grew rich from fitting out ships for the Saint-Malo corsairs and taking their share of the plunder. Out to sea is a constantly changing panorama – the clustered masts of the marina, the houses of Dinard across the estuary, the bastion of Cap Fréhel far away to the west, the little offshore islands and jagged reefs that make navigation into Saint-Malo so hazardous.

Spaced round the ramparts are statues of three of Saint-Malo's most famous seafarers, the corsairs Duguay-Trouin and Surcouf, and the explorer Jacques Cartier. If his periwigged statue is anything to go by, René Duguay-Trouin was a rather dandified figure – but his career was anything but dandified. Born in 1673, he commanded his first ship at the age of 18, and by the time he was 36 had captured 300 merchant ships, mainly English and Dutch, and thirty men-of-war. The high point of his career came in 1711, when he took Rio de Janeiro from the Portuguese and rescued a French expeditionary force held captive there. After this exploit he hardly ever put to sea again. He died in 1736, and was buried in Saint-Malo cathedral, leaving behind him a reputation as a fine commander and a chivalrous enemy.

The Saint-Malo corsairs were not pirates in the generally accepted sense of the word. On the contrary, they were legitimate agents of the French crown, acting under official licence. Merchants, *armateurs* and captains who wished to fit out ships to *faire la course* (hence the word 'corsair') had to obtain the sanction of the Ministry of Marine Affairs, followed by Letters of Marque signed by the King (in Duguay-Trouin's case, Louis XIV), which allowed citizens to equip a ship with arms in order to attack enemy vessels. Once at sea, definite rules were laid down. A corsair was not allowed to pillage or sink his prize, but had to seal her hatches and sail her back to port, taking her captain and crew on board his own vessel (no walking the plank here). On their return to harbour, ship and cargo were sold. One-tenth went to the Crown; of the remainder, two-thirds went to the *armateur*, while the remaining third was divided between captain, officers and crew, the captain naturally getting the largest share.

On the opposite side of the ramparts, Saint-Malo's other great corsair, Robert Surcouf, gestures menacingly in the general direction of England. Born exactly a century after Duguay-Trouin, Surcouf won glory during the Napoleonic wars. He got his first command in 1794, when he was only 20, and gave up active seafaring some fifteen years later. His greatest triumph came in 1800, when his sleek privateer, the *Confiance*, captured a huge East Indiaman, the *Kent*, in the Bay of Bengal. Following the rules of *la course*, Surcouf sailed his prize back to Port-Louis in Mauritius, which at that time belonged to the French. The authorities claimed their share of the gold dust carried in barrels on the *Kent*; whereupon the enraged Surcouf, who had hoped to reward his sailors with the booty, had the barrels tipped into the sea, and told the officials to go and pick the gold off the bottom themselves. After his retirement Surcouf grew prosperous as an *armateur* in the slave trade. He died in 1827 and was buried with military honours in Saint-Malo cemetery.

As a postscript to the Surcouf story, a few years ago, in the small museum at Mahébourg in Mauritius, I came across reminders of his exploits – a portrait of Surcouf, his pistol, and a case of relics from the *Kent*, including her captain's telescope and sword. Mahébourg's name as well as its museum has Saint-Malo links: it comes from Bertrand Mahé de la Bourdonnais, who was born in Saint-Malo in 1699, and governed Mauritius in the mid eighteenth century.

Half-way round the ramparts, and equidistant between the two corsairs, is a rugged statue comme-

*Tall granite houses, built originally by wealthy eighteenth-century shipowners, loom above the massive ramparts of Saint-Malo.*

morating a more peaceable Saint-Malo sea-dog. Between 1534 and 1541 Jacques Cartier made three epic voyages across the Atlantic, hoping to find a western route to the fabulous wealth of India and Cathay. Like Columbus before him, he failed; but in the process he discovered Canada, and made his way up the Saint Lawrence River as far as the present site of Montreal. He retired to Rothéneuf, just outside Saint-Malo, and died there heavily in debt in 1557.

At almost any stage of the rampart walk you can step down into the little town – 'smaller than the Tuileries gardens' as the writer François-René de Chateaubriand, born in Saint-Malo in 1768, described it. His birthplace is now the Hôtel de France et Chateaubriand, facing the castle across the Place Chateaubriand; a rambling house with a pretty central courtyard, it is typical of the mansions built by prosperous *armateurs*. Chateaubriand is commemorated elsewhere in Saint-Malo by a statue in front of the casino; and he is buried on the Grand Bé, one of Saint-Malo's offshore islands, which you can reach on foot across the sand at low tide. He had already chosen his last resting-place before his death in 1848. The previous year the novelist Gustave Flaubert, who was greatly influenced by Chateaubriand, visited the site and wrote in floridly Romantic terms: 'He will sleep with his head turned towards the sea; in this tomb built upon a reef, his immortality will be like his life, deserted by his fellows and surrounded by storms.' His tomb bears no name – just the inscription *un grand écrivain français*.

Saint-Malo's massive fifteenth-century château stands at the north-eastern corner of the town, adjoining the main walls but outside them. It was built by the dukes of Brittany primarily to keep control of the headstrong and independent-minded Malouins, rather than to defend them from outside attack. An old saying sums up their pride in their birthplace: *Malouin d'abord, breton peut-être, français s'il en reste* ('A Saint-Malo man first, a Breton perhaps, a Frenchman if anything is left over').

One of the towers, the Grand Donjon, is now a museum telling the seafaring history of the town from medieval times through to World War II and the present day; another, the Quic-en-Groigne, houses a collection of waxwork tableaux, largely devoted to lurid reconstructions of the exploits of the corsairs. The latter's strange name stems from a remark by Duchess Anne, who built it about 1500. When the Malouins complained about its strength, she replied *Qui qu'en groigne, ainsi sera: tel est mon bon plaisir* ('Complain as much as you like, that is how it will be: such is my desire'). So that the Malouins did not miss the point of her words, she had them carved on the tower's outer wall.

The name of the Venelle des Chiens (Dog Lane) not far from the castle, recalls the guard dogs that in earlier centuries roamed outside the town walls from sunset to sunrise. These *chiens du guet* (watchdogs) or *dogues* were mastiffs of English stock, described by a sixteenth-century traveller as 'the most savage and furious dogs a man could see anywhere'. They were finally retired in 1770, after they had savaged to death a young naval officer returning late at night from a visit to his fiancée in Saint-Servan. They still live on, though only in emblematic form: if you look up at the Saint-Malo flag fluttering from the castle tower, you can see a *dogue* portrayed in one corner.

The main building of Saint-Malo Intra-Muros ('Within the Walls'), as the inner town is called, is St Vincent's Cathedral, still so called though it is no longer the seat of a bishop. The vaulted nave dates from the twelfth century, while the chancel, well lit by tall windows and supported on slender columns, was built a century later. Outside is one of the prettiest corners of Saint-Malo – a fragment of a cloister built against the cathedral wall.

On its eastern side Saint-Malo shades into the resort-suburb of Paramé, which gives way to the quieter, family-oriented Rothéneuf. It is worth stopping here for a look at the extraordinary Rochers Sculptés, a

---

*The islet of Petit Bé, with its seventeenth-century fort, is one of a chain of rocky islands that guard the approaches to the port of Saint-Malo.*

*A medieval font decorated with crudely carved human figures in Saint-Malo Cathedral.*

phantasmagoria of rock carvings hacked out of a granite headland. For 25 years towards the end of the last century a clerical recluse, the Abbé Fourier, worked away at his portrait gallery of the Rothéneuf family of corsairs, along with assorted saints, devils, sailors, peasants and sea-monsters. Every year their faces become more blurred through the action of wind and wave, and even more from the footwear of the thousands of summer visitors who tramp round the Abbé's creations.

Beyond Rothéneuf, a country road (D201) passes large granite farmhouses which as likely as not began life in the seventeenth or eighteenth century as *malouinières* – country houses built by *armateurs* or corsairs. The road ends at a hotel on the Pointe du Grouin, the headland that marks the western limit of the Baie du Mont-Saint-Michel. Across a narrow chasm is the long ridgeback of the Ile des Landes, now a

nature reserve and bird sanctuary, loud with squabbling gulls and cormorants.

South of Grouin is Cancale, the mecca of oyster-fanciers on the north Breton coast. Cancale is a double town: from the modern church and supermarkets of its upper half, a steep hill leads down to the harbour, and the quayside above the muddy foreshore. The lower town consists largely of restaurants, cafés and bars where you can eat your fill of oysters; or you can sample a few a good deal more cheaply from open-air oyster stalls, mainly run by weatherbeaten old ladies.

Oysters have been grown in the rich silt of the bay for centuries. By the seventeenth century they had such a high reputation that Louis XIV had cartloads of them sent up to Versailles from Cancale; and a century later Casanova was wolfing down fifty an evening to keep up his strength for the night's activities. These were the large oysters called *pieds de cheval* because they are shaped like a horse's hoof. Next in quality are the *plates*, or flat oysters, also known as *bélons*, from the Bélon estuary in Finistère where fine oysters still grow; and lowest in the scale are the *creuses* (hollow oysters), most of which originate from Japan.

A couple of kilometres offshore are the *parcs*, where the oysters grow to maturity in *poches* – sacks of plastic mesh, attached in rows to metal frames fastened in the shallows. When they have become large enough to be edible, they are collected in flat-bottomed punts, brought back to Cancale, and transferred to the stone tanks that line the foreshore, where they clean themselves internally, getting rid of their impurities in mud-free water. Only after they are clean inside and out are they considered fit for the table. Oysters are normally eaten at three or four years old. The breeding season takes place during the warm weather from May until August, which presumably accounts for the belief that oysters should only be eaten when there is an R in the month.

*Rock fingers on the Pointe du Grouin, the headland that marks the western limit of the bay of Mont-Saint-Michel.*

Some years ago I spent an exhausting day out in the *parcs* with an oysterman and his crew. The work, carried out at low tide, consisted mainly of turning the *poches* to make sure the oysters were evenly spread, and hitting the green crabs that prey on them. It does not sound like particularly heavy work; but what made it backbreaking was the sheer number of the *poches* and the glutinous quality of the tidal *vase* or mud, which turned every step I took into a struggle against being sucked ankle-deep into the slime.

Cancale is a fishing port as well as an oyster-growing centre. Until half a century ago its fishermen put to sea in the traditional Breton fishing-boat — the chunky *bisquine*, 17m in length, with square mainsail, long bowsprit and huge triangular spinnaker. During the summer, you can take a trip from Cancale in a modern *bisquine*, built a few years ago to the old specifications. Cancale's fishing and oyster-growing history is brought to life in the Musée des Arts et Traditions Populaires, housed in a converted church.

South and east from Cancale, the road skirts the Bay of Mont-Saint-Michel through Saint-Benoît-des-Ondes and Le Vivier-sur-Mer. *Vivier* is the French for fishpond, and it is no coincidence that Le Vivier is one of France's main mussel-growing centres. Le Vivier is rightly proud of its wheeled amphibian, the *Sirène de la Baie*, which takes 150 passengers around and on the water of the bay for two-hour trips, devouring oysters and mussels as they admire the distant view of the abbey of Mont-Saint-Michel, rising through the sea-haze like a scene from some medieval Book of Hours. (Though Mont-Saint-Michel is technically in Normandy, and thus outside the scope of this book, no one visiting this part of Brittany should pass it by, as it is one of Europe's architectural marvels.)

Here and there along this stretch of road you pass the towers of abandoned windmills, which must have given the coast something of a Dutch look in the days when they still had sails twirling away. The reclaimed land towards Mont-Saint-Michel is known as *polder*, a name no doubt given by drainage engineers brought in from Holland.

Until the eighth century the huge 'C' of the bay was dry land, covered in the trees of the Forest of Scissy (the Roman Sessiacum), and dotted with villages in the clearings. But in 709 or thereabouts an immense tidal wave swept in from the Atlantic, engulfing the forest, drowning the villages, and leaving a folk memory of church bells tolling where the boats now chug out to the oyster-beds. Though the villages have been under the water for almost 1300 years, the names of several of them are known from records — Tommen, Porspican, La Feuilleste, Saint-Louis and half a dozen more.

Through Le Vivier the road swings inland towards Dol-de-Bretagne, 8 kilometres to the south. Above the drained salt-marshes of the Marais de Dol, now some of the richest farmland in Brittany, rises the flat-topped granite outcrop of Mont-Dol, which in this featureless landscape has a scenic importance out of all proportion to its height of only 65m. *Dol* is Breton for 'table', and Mont-Dol means simply 'Table Mountain'. It was a holy place in Celtic, pre-Christian days, and its sanctity was maintained by the early Christians, who established hermitages on it. Like many such high places where Christianity came into conflict with earlier beliefs, it was claimed as the battleground between St Michael, who left his footprint in a rock on the summit, and the Devil, who left his claw-mark.

The flat top of the hill is crowned by a tall tower, dated 1837, which formed the base of a statue of the Virgin. She was blown down and shattered in a storm in 1989, but there are hopes that she will eventually be replaced. Near the tower is a tiny chapel, while elsewhere on the summit are the remains of two windmills, and the foundations of a so-called 'temple of Mithras'. At the end of the eighteenth century Mont-Dol was one of the chain of 55 telegraph stations between Paris and Napoleon's naval headquarters at Brest. Messages were transmitted by means of a semaphore system of pivoted wooden arms; though

*Flat farmland stretches northwards from Mont-Dol towards the bay of Mont-Saint-Michel. Reclaimed centuries ago from the sea by Dutch engineers, the fields are still known as* polders.

*A grotesque wooden figure adorns a medieval shop-front in the Grande Rue des Stuarts, Dol-de-Bretagne.*

the chain was useless at night or in fog, it remained in operation until it was superseded by the electric telegraph in the 1840s.

Dol is one of the prettiest little towns in north Brittany. Its main street, the Grande Rue des Stuarts, consists largely of medieval granite houses, balanced on stumpy stone pillars and crowned by crazily angled gables. It no doubt gets its name from the Stuart King James II, who fled to France after the 'Glorious Revolution' of 1688. In summer, the grey stone is brightened by hanging flower-baskets and window-boxes, and coloured bunting stretched from side to side of the street.

Until the French Revolution Dol was the seat of a bishopric. The cathedral, tucked away in a square behind the Grande Rue, is a nobly austere building on the largest scale. Dedicated to St Samson and built mainly in the thirteenth century, it has a strangely asymmetrical west front, with two towers, one of which looks as though a giant hand had snapped its top off; this was begun in the sixteenth century but never completed. The other tower is a century older, and is said to be connected to Mont-Dol by an underground passage. The gothic south porch, built in the four-teenth and fifteenth centuries, is huge, and the magnificent nave soars to a vaulted ceiling twenty metres above the floor. The eighty superb oak choir stalls are fifteenth-century, and are carved with foliage and human heads. The windows still have some of their medieval stained glass, illustrating episodes from the life of St Samson of Dol.

Brittany claims to have no fewer than 7847 saints: a strange-looking number, which is in fact the sum total of seven thousand, seven hundred, seven score and seven. As one of Brittany's Sept Saints Fondateurs ('Seven Founding Saints'), St Samson is at the top of the sanctity league, along with Saints Malo, Brieuc, Tugdual, Paul-Aurélian (usually shortened to Pol), Corentin and Patern.

We know more about Samson than any of the rest of them, from an anonymous biography believed to have been written at the beginning of the seventh century. He was probably born about 490, in North Wales, and was educated at the monastery of Llantwit, in Glamor-gan, one of the leading Welsh seats of learning. After missionary work in Ireland, at the age of 30 or so he was 'commanded in a vision' to preach the Gospel beyond the seas, and crossed the Bristol Channel to Cornwall. Here he did his best to convert the Bretons to Christianity by preaching, performing miracles and carving crosses on the standing stones they worship-ped. From Cornwall he made his way across the Channel to Brittany, where according to one account he landed at Le Vivier in 548.

*The low crossing tower and southern side of St Samson's Cathedral, Dol-de-Bretagne, built mainly in the thirteenth century.*

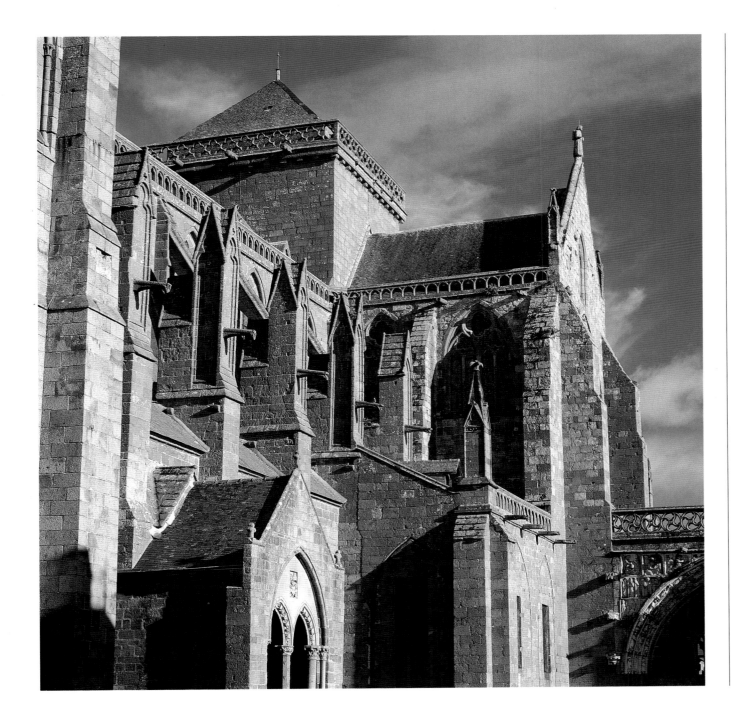

Arriving in Dol, he founded a monastery, and (according to his biographer) 'planted the seed of many works of a wonderful character, and founded many monasteries throughout almost the entire province'. As Bishop of Dol he fell foul of Childebert I, King of the Franks, or at least of his queen Ultrogoth, who tried to get rid of him by giving him poison, having him thrown from a wild horse, and setting a lion on him. None of these attempts succeeded: the poisoned chalice broke in the cupbearer's hand, while Samson tamed the horse with the sign of the Cross and killed the lion by calling on Christ and hurling javelins at it. This was too much for Ultrogoth, who suffered an apoplectic fit and died on the spot, leaving Samson to carry on his work unmolested. He died around 570, though this date is as uncertain as that of his birth.

Samson and the other missionary-bishops of the early Celtic church were tough men of action, quite unlike the peaceable clerics who wear the bishop's mitre today. They went about armed in a violent society; their monasteries were fortresses as well as refuges from the world's temptations; and in appearance they bore more resemblance to Mohican warriors than to the round-tonsured monks of later centuries, as they cut their hair in the 'Johannes tonsure', shaving it from ear to ear and leaving it long at the back. No doubt the simple pagan peasants of Cornwall and Brittany found it easier to be led by such men than to resist them.

To see a superb example of the 'idols' on which Samson and his like carved their crosses, drive a kilometre along the D795 in the direction of Combourg. Down a lane on the left is the Menhir du Champ Dolent, a standing stone more than 9m high and one of the most impressive such stones in Brittany. (As a matter of terminology, a menhir is a single standing stone, from the Breton *men*, stone, and *hir*, long; while a dolmen – literally 'table stone' – consists of two uprights and a horizontal laid across them.) According to legend, it is sinking into the earth at the rate of a couple of centimetres a century, and when it finally disappears the world will come to an end. This gives the earth another half a million years or so still to go.

The name Champ Dolent probably derives from the Latin *campus dolensis*, 'field of Dol', but is usually given a more fanciful origin as the 'field of grief', its French meaning. The story goes that two brothers and their armies were engaged in a ferocious battle here, so hard fought that enough blood flowed from the dead and wounded to drive a watermill. When the battle was at its height, the stone fell from the sky and embedded itself in the ground between the opposing forces. After this signal of divine disapproval, the brothers sensibly called off the battle.

Leaving the menhir, continue along the D795 to Combourg. On the far side of this compact little medieval town is the turreted château, buried among the trees of a magnificent park and standing above a wide lake, where Chateaubriand spent his pre-revolutionary childhood. The original castle was built by the Bishop of Dol in the eleventh century, though the present building, with its romantically pointed turrets and massive walls, is mainly fifteenth-century.

Chateaubriand has left an account of his boyhood at Combourg in his brilliant autobiography *Mémoires d'Outre-Tombe* (*Memoirs from Beyond the Grave*), written at intervals throughout his life and completed only in 1846, two years before his death. He lived with his terrifying old father the Vicomte, his mother and his adored elder sister Lucile in an atmosphere of claustrophobic intensity. His bedroom was in an isolated turret known as the Tour du Chat, from the skeleton of a cat found under the stairs and shown to visitors. In the *Mémoires*, he recalls the ghost of an early Count of Combourg, who had a wooden leg and was sometimes encountered on the stairs with a black cat at his heels.

Although fear of ghosts, owls, rays of the moon and strange noises from below terrified him alone in his tower,'this harsh way of treating me left me with the

*The abbey of Mont-Saint-Michel is a constant feature of the view across the bay as you take the coast road from Cancale to Le Vivier. Brittany lost the abbey to Normandy when the River Couesnon changed its course.*

courage of a man, without depriving me of that sensitivity of imagination of which they nowadays try to deprive young people'. Perhaps it was not such a bad upbringing for one of the high priests of Romanticism, who in works like the novel *Atala*, praising the virtues of the savage life, was an inspiration to Flaubert, Victor Hugo and a host of lesser writers.

From Combourg, take cross-country roads through La Chapelle-aux-Fitzméens to the village of Pleugueneuc. On its outskirts is the Château de la Bourbansais, reached down a long drive lined with beech trees. Built in various styles from the sixteenth to the eighteenth century, it is a typically dour Breton château, symmetrical and solid, and flanked by separate pavilions. Inside there is fine eighteenth-century panelling, and the gardens are laid out in the formal French style. During the eighteenth century it belonged to the Huard family, who for generations were members of the Etats – the semi-independent Parliament of Brittany, which met periodically at Rennes, and was abolished at the Revolution. La Bourbansais has a small open-air zoo in its park; more unusually, it also has its own pack of hounds.

Head next for Dinan. As you near the town, its church towers and roofline come into view across the deep valley of the Rance. Far below, beside the river, is the old port, one of the most picturesque in Brittany, which appears briefly on the right from the high-level viaduct that leads to the upper town. The road swings past Dinan's feudal castle into the main square, where a statue of Bertrand du Guesclin sits commandingly on horseback among the parked cars.

Dinan is the quintessence of Brittany's medieval towns, and its ancient half-timbered buildings and general air of timelessness have been enticing tourists for 150 years or more. In 1839 Thomas Adolphus Trollope, the novelist's elder brother, visited Dinan

*The fifteenth-century turrets of the Château de Combourg are reflected in its ornamental lake. The writer Chateaubriand spent his childhood in the castle, which he claimed was haunted.*

*Half-timbering and cobblestones in the Rue du Jerzual help to give Dinan its reputation as 'the quintessence of Brittany's medieval towns'.*

and found it a tax haven of the 1830s, at a time when the English were the financial lords of Europe. Dinan, he wrote, was 'one of those towns which have become colonies of English emigrants. It is very pretty and conveniently situated, and was very cheap; and so a tribe of our wandering countrymen marked it for their own. . . . At Dinan you may live very comfortably at a tolerable hotel for £3 a month.' Today you would be lucky to get away with less than a hundred times that amount – or two hundred, if meals are included. Fortunately, other things in Dinan have remained much the same since Trollope's day, notably its prettiness and convenient situation.

Medieval Dinan stretches along a ridge above the river, with streets of gabled houses dropping steeply down to the Rance waterfront. From the Place Du Guesclin it is only a couple of hundred metres to the

*Bertrand du Guesclin, commander-in-chief of the French army during the fourteenth century, was renowned for his ugliness as well his bravery. He was born near Dinan in about 1320.*

Jardin Anglais, the town's biggest and best open space, where the English connection lives on, in name at least. This grassy expanse is planted in the informal ('English' to the French) style, with a wide-spreading cedar, a tall ginkgo, a large magnolia, and other fine specimen trees. It gives a wonderful panorama of the port, the Rance and the heights on the opposite side of the river. Beside one of the garden walks is the dignified bust of the explorer Auguste Pavie, who was born in Dinan in 1847. Employed as a young man by the French-run telegraph company in Cambodia, he spent five years drawing up a map of the country, finally becoming head of the geographical service in French Indo-China. He retired to a village in Ille-et-Vilaine, where he died in 1925.

In former centuries the garden was the burial-ground of Dinan's principal church, the Basilique Saint-Sauveur. Basically a twelfth-century roman-esque building, it was largely rebuilt in the fifteenth and sixteenth centuries, with a three-storey bell tower added in the seventeenth century. Worth looking out for are the winged animals that flank the romanesque west doorway. Inside there are some remarkable treasures – a twelfth-century font, a fifteenth-century stained-glass window of the four evangelists, and, in the north transept, a shrine to Du Guesclin, which contains the general's heart, removed from his body and buried here after he died on a campaign in 1380.

Throughout Brittany you will find streets, hotels and bars named after Du Guesclin. But he has a special connection with Dinan, as he was born near by, in the Château de la Motte-Broons, about 1320. As a child he was remarkably plain; a troubadour called Cuvelier wrote of him: 'I believe that there was no child so ugly from Rennes to Dinan. He was snub-nosed and swarthy, scowling and stocky; his father and mother hated him so much that they often wished him dead or drowned in running water.' No doubt his early battles against parental hostility turned him into a fighter.

Du Guesclin first came to prominence at the age of 18, at a tournament held in Rennes, when he borrowed a horse and armour, and proceeded to unseat one knight after another, until his own helmet was knocked off and the crowd saw his beetle-browed face. The Hundred Years War – or that part of it that affected the duchy of Brittany, claimed by both England and France – suited his talents, and for the next twenty years or so he fought up and down the country. His most famous encounter took place at Dinan in the 1350s, when he fought a single-handed tournament with an English knight, Sir Thomas Canterbury. After fighting with lance and sword, Du

*A narrow medieval bridge crosses the River Rance at Dinan's own small port, below the upper town. A new, high-level bridge takes the strain of modern traffic.*

Guesclin nearly killed Canterbury by smashing him in the face with his mailed fist.

The final phase of his career had a wider stage, on the battlefields of Spain and southern France. Appointed Constable (commander-in-chief) of France by Charles V, he died on a campaign against the English in 1380, while besieging a town in the Massif Central. In the macabre medieval fashion, his body was dispersed across half of France: his entrails were buried at Le Puy in the Massif Central; his flesh was boiled from the bones and buried at Clermont-Ferrand; his skeleton was buried at Saint-Dénis, necropolis of the French kings on the outskirts of Paris; and his heart was placed in a silver casket and taken back to Dinan.

Almost every building in old Dinan is worth a look, and can be seen in comfort, as much of the centre is pedestrianized. From the Jardin Anglais, you can take the zigzag footpath down to the Rance and stroll by the river to the old harbour and medieval bridge. Then walk up the ancient Rue du Petit Fort between gabled half-timbered houses, through the fortified Porte du Jerzual and up the street of the same name to the Place des Cordeliers (Square of the Leather-Workers) in the heart of the old town.

Just west of the Place des Cordeliers, in the Grand' Rue, is Dinan's second ancient church. Dedicated to St Malo and built in Flamboyant gothic style, it was begun in the fifteenth century but not completed until 1865. The twin-arched renaissance entrance porch, which dates from the early seventeenth century, is elegantly carved with slender pilasters and scallop shells. It leads into a fine though neglected-looking interior, with tall gothic arches and a soaring apsidal east end. The unusual stained glass, mainly from the 1920s, tells the story of Dinan's early history, including lively scenes featuring Du Guesclin, Duchess Anne and other notables. A large oil painting shows the chief

religious event in the church's history – the translation in 1670 of the relics of St Malo from Saint-Malo to Dinan.

The spine of medieval Dinan is the Rue de l'Horloge; its name comes from a fifteenth-century clock tower, well worth the 60-metre climb for the spectacular view from the top. The Tourist Office near by is in a grand sixteenth-century town house, the Hôtel Kératry. Just opposite is a gabled medieval house perched on dumpy granite pillars. Known as the 'Maison du Gisant', it gets its name from a battered tomb-effigy (*gisant*), dressed in armour, on the pavement below the arcade. In the fifteenth century the house was the workshop of an effigy sculptor, who mass-produced such tomb furniture for the churches round about, carving standard bodies, and then adding heads and coats of arms to order. This unobtrusive statue might seem out of place in most other towns, but looks just right in the centre of Dinan, where the Middle Ages still seem a living reality. Across the Place Du Guesclin, at the south-west angle of the town walls, is the medieval castle, known as the Château de la Duchesse Anne after the last duchess of an independent Brittany. The main tower, built in the fourteenth century, contains a small local-history museum.

As you would expect in a town crammed with ancient buildings, Dinan has more than its fair share of antique shops. If you want a bargain, avoid the tourist trap streets like the Rue du Jerzual and the Rue du Petit Fort, and hunt around the alleys of the old town, or look outside the medieval town wall in the more recently built shopping streets.

A kilometre south of Dinan, a back road leads to Léhon Abbey, beside the Rance; there is also a riverside path. The abbey was founded in the ninth century by six monks who stole the relics of St Magloire, Bishop of Dol, from the island of Sark, and transferred them to their new monastery. The present church is thirteenth-century, and has what is believed to be the oldest stained glass in Brittany.

From Dinan, head west along the Lamballe road (N176), and then veer north-west towards Plancoët (D794). Shortly before the village of Corseul, a ruined

---

*Vigorously carved renaissance detail distinguishes the twin-arched southern doorway of Dinan's church of Saint-Malo, a fine building in Flamboyant gothic style.*

tower, which looks as if it could be anything from medieval to nineteenth-century, stands isolated in the middle of the fields. Known as the Temple of Mars, this battered fragment is Brittany's most important Gallo-Roman survival. It probably dates from the first century AD, when Brittany was the province of Gallia Armorica on the western fringes of the Roman Empire. The remains, made of a double skin of small granite bricks with stone rubble filling between, look like part of an octagonal apse from some much larger building. In spite of its name, it is not certain whether it was a temple at all, though it may have been a *cella* or sanctuary, or whether it had anything to do with Mars.

Corseul's name derives from a pre-Roman tribe, the Curiosolites, conquered by Julius Caesar in 56 BC. Though today's village is hardly worth a second glance, in Roman times it was a major regional centre, with a forum, temples and public baths, burnt down around AD 400. For centuries the site was plundered for its stone; as recently as the eighteenth century some was removed to strengthen the walls of Saint-Malo.

Up the road is Plancoët, a small up-and-down town on the River Arguenon. As a boy towards the end of the eighteenth century, Chateaubriand used to visit his grandmother there, and describes her house and garden in his autobiography. Nowadays Plancoët provides much of Brittany's mineral water. From Plancoët, continue westwards to Lamballe along the minor D28, which wanders cross-country through the forest of La Hunaudaie. South of the road, past Pléven village, are the ruined walls and turrets of La Hunaudaie castle, built mainly in the fourteenth and fifteenth centuries, and blown up during the French Revolution. Restoration work is now under way.

Though Lamballe is only 10 kilometres inland from the seaside resorts of the Côte d'Emeraude, it is still very much a working town, rather than a holiday centre. It is said to have been founded in the sixth century by St Pol, the name Lamballe coming from 'Lan Pol' ('Pol's Monastery'). During the Middle Ages it was the capital of the Duchy of Penthièvre, one of Brittany's most important subdivisions, and was much fought over. In more recent centuries it became a centre for tanning and leather-working.

The old town centre runs along a ridge above the valley of the Gouessant, and is bounded by two major churches, the fifteenth-century Saint-Jean on the west, and the twelfth-century Notre Dame de Grande Puissance ('Our Lady of Great Power') on the east. Between the two is the long Place du Martray ('Graveyard Square'), which has most of Lamballe's old houses. The tourist office is in one of the finest of these half-timbered buildings, the Maison du Bourreau ('Hangman's House'). Upstairs is a museum devoted to the paintings and drawings of Mathurin Méheut (1882–1958), who was born in Lamballe, and spent most of his long artistic career recording the fast-vanishing farming and seafaring life of his native Brittany, dashing off sketches of everyday scenes such as fishermen mending their nets, or women seated at table, with a few rapid strokes of pencil or charcoal.

Lamballe is renowned throughout North France for its Haras National (National Stud Farm), founded as long ago as 1825. The stables, which house rows of stallions in individual stalls, are built round an enormous sanded yard, the Cour d'Honneur. The stud breeds mainly Breton draught horses (the immensely strong and docile Trait Breton), and trotting horses.

A family of Breton noblemen, the Princes de Lamballe, took their hereditary title from the town. At the time of the French Revolution, the current Princesse de Lamballe was a close friend of Marie-Antoinette. She was guillotined in September 1792, and her head was brandished on a pike outside the prison where the Queen was held. Just over a year later, Marie-Antoinette too went to the guillotine.

Head north along the D791 to the small resort of Le Val-André, westernmost of the resorts of the Côte d'Emeraude, whose wide sandy beaches have been north Brittany's holiday playground for well over a century. Le Val-André's seafront beach is as good as

*Romanesque heads decorate granite capitals in the church of Notre Dame de Grande Puissance, Lamballe.*

any of them; and its little port of Dahouët, which once sent a cod-fishing fleet to the waters off Iceland, is now a safe anchorage for small pleasure craft.

From Le Val-André the D786 runs east along the coast to Erquy. Half-way between the two is one of the most delightful small châteaux I know, the Château de Bienassis, whose name (meaning 'well-sited') is more than justified. Reached down long tree-lined avenues, it is a neat little fortified manor-house, built in the fifteenth century with moat and pointed turrets, and surrounded by formal gardens where bees murmur on hot summer afternoons. It was largely burnt down in the religious wars of the sixteenth century, and saw violence as recently as World War II, when the Germans shot six local inhabitants in what is now the rose garden.

The little fishing port of Erquy is the perfect place to sit at a waterfront bar, watching the boats bobbing idly in the harbour. Its small fishing fleet lives from its catches of scallops (*coquilles-Saint-Jacques*). The harbour is guarded on the north by a magnificent headland, the Cap d'Erquy, which rises sheer from the sea for 68m. Its summit was fortified by local tribesmen in the Iron Age, though the defensive ditches are often attributed to Caesar. Virtually every little lane round Erquy leads down to a fine beach.

Continuing east from Erquy, take the D34 through Sables-d'Or-les-Pins to Cap Fréhel. Sables-d'Or is a shapeless, unfinished-seeming family resort, with no proper centre, and consisting almost entirely of hotels and seaside cottages. Yet it fully lives up to its name, as its beaches are vast and golden, and the hills on either side are covered in pine trees. One miraculous evening I saw a school of porpoises leaping in the sea off Sables-d'Or as the sun went down; but that was in the days before over-fishing had depleted the fish stocks, and there was plenty for porpoises as well as human beings. I will always have a special affection for Sables-d'Or, as for years we went on family camping holidays to the hamlet of Vieux-Bourg, on the way to Cap Fréhel. The campsite, on pine-covered dunes, was rough and ready; but within a few metres of our tent was an enormous sandy beach.

Cap Fréhel is the most spectacular headland on the north coast of Brittany. Towering 70m above the waves which crash on the rocks below, it is clearly visible across the sea from Saint-Malo, more than 20 kilometres away. In the days of the corsairs, Saint-Malo sailors were supposed to keep their marriage vows until they had rounded Fréhel's mighty rampart; but once they were west of it, they were absolved from monogamy until their return. There has been a lighthouse here for centuries; beside the slender modern tower, built in 1950, is a squat square strucutre which dates from the seventeenth century. On a clear day, the view from the top of the modern lighthouse (open daily in summer except in bad weather) extends from the Cherbourg peninsula in the east to the Ile de Bréhat in the west – a seascape of more than 50 kilometres.

The wild heathland on the crest of the cape is a nature reserve; while the pinkish-grey sandstone cliffs, falling away to a chaos of rocks along the shore, are a bird sanctuary for gulls, cormorants, seamews and guillemots, which nest in the crevices or wheel screaming above the sea. All over the Fréhel heathland you will find relics of the German occupation during World War II – concrete gun emplacements, trenches and earthworks, and sloping ramps leading down to silos, which presumably were launching platforms for flying bombs or rockets.

The Fréhel peninsula is really a double cape, with twin promontories. East of the lighthouse, across a rocky bay, is the Pointe de la Latte, separated from the mainland by a deep gorge. This natural strongpoint is the dramatic setting for Fort La Latte, an impregnable-looking castle built in the thirteenth and fourteenth centuries, and adapted in the late seventeenth century for artillery. When I first went there a good many years ago, I was mystified by a medieval-style wheeled

*Daffodils colour the formal gardens of the Château de Bienassis, near Le Val-André. The fortified manor house was built in the fifteenth century.*

battering ram and some crude-looking carts in and around the castle. The mystery was cleared up a year or two later, when I saw the 1950s Kirk Douglas/Tony Curtis epic *The Vikings*, filmed partly at Fort La Latte.

From Cap Fréhel round to Saint-Malo the coast is cut by a succession of estuaries, whose sandbars and mudflats, uncovered at low tide, are happy hunting-grounds for lovers of crabs and shellfish. Just past the first of these estuaries is Matignon, on the D786; the town gets its name from a prominent local family, who also gave their name to the Hôtel de Matignon, one of the great mansions of Paris. From Matignon, head north on the D13 to Saint-Cast, a typical seaside resort sprawling across the end of a peninsula. High above the town is a monument commemorating the Battle of Saint-Cast, which took place in 1758 during the Seven Years War, and ended in defeat for a combined English and Welsh invading force. Erected in 1858 to celebrate the centenary of the battle, it consists of a column surmounted by a rusty cast-iron sculpture group, which portrays the Breton greyhound trampling on the British lion.

The battle gave rise to a legend which may well have its origins in truth, no doubt somewhat garbled; at any rate, it confirms the strength of Celtic solidarity. The story goes that a company of Breton troops were marching into battle against a detachment of Welsh infantry, who were singing one of their national songs. The Bretons suddenly halted, recognizing it as one of their own country tunes, and began to bellow out the chorus. The Welsh halted in their turn; then, throwing down their weapons in defiance of their officers, Welshmen and Bretons fell on one another's necks.

The Battle of Saint-Cast also produced an epigram which was far from complimentary to the Duc d'Aiguillon, the French commander-in-chief. He kept an eye on the progress of the battle from the safe vantage-point of a nearby windmill, which gave rise to the saying: 'The French army was covered in glory, and the Duc d'Aiguillon in flour'. Whatever his abilities as a military commander, he was practical enough; from about 1755, as governor of Brittany, he laid out the region's road system along its present lines, and later became Louis XV's minister of foreign affairs.

Back on the D786, you cross the Arguenon estuary past the village of Notre Dame du Guildo. A little way downstream on the far bank, you can make out the ruined towers of a medieval castle, with its foundations in the estuary mud and its battlements among the trees. Today it is hard to envisage the castle as it was in the days of its glory, as it is the kind of ruin where an owl flies into your face as you fight your way towards it through the undergrowth. Though the castle of Le Guildo is not officially open to the public, it is worth turning up the side-road for a closer look, as it was the home of one of the most luridly melodramatic characters of medieval Brittany, Prince Gilles de Bretagne, youngest son of Duke Jean V. Born in 1424, he was brought up at the English court, where he became thoroughly anglicized and surrounded himself with English cronies. Back at Le Guildo, he hired an English garrison, sent for his London friends, and engaged in a riotous lifestyle. (The French expression, *courir le guilledou*, which has the dictionary meaning 'to frequent places of ill-fame', is said to date back to the debauchery of Gilles and his friends.)

However, his eventual downfall was due not to his immorality but to his meddling in politics, notably to suspicions that he was plotting with Henry VI of England to usurp the dukedom of Brittany from his elder brother, Duke François I. In 1446 François had Gilles arrested, and for the next four years he was shunted from one Brittany castle to another, suffering increasingly harsh treatment, and was finally murdered in the grim fortress of Le Hardouinais, in the centre of Brittany, at the instigation of Duke François — or so contemporary opinion reckoned. A group of Gilles's enemies hired four assassins to carry out the deed; after poisoning him and half strangling him, they finally suffocated him under a mattress. He was just 26.

*Fort La Latte, a medieval castle later adapted for the age of artillery, dominates its impregnable site by the sea near Cap Fréhel.*

Duke François survived Gilles by less than three months, tormented by guilt for his younger brother's death, and possibly poisoned in his turn. The following year the four murderers were brought to justice. They were decapitated, and their bodies were quartered and displayed on scaffolds. Ironically, the wild boy of Brittany's ducal family achieved a near-saintly posthumous reputation, and miracles were reported to have taken place at his tomb in Boquen Abbey, 20 kilometres south of Lamballe.

Carrying on round the coast, the D786 brings you by way of the lesser resorts of Lancieux and Saint-Briac to Dinard, queen of the Côte d'Emeraude. In spite of a few gestures in the direction of modernity, Dinard preserves an atmosphere of sedate pre-war elegance. It is north Brittany's most sophisticated seaside resort, and has something for everybody – broad sandy beaches, hotels ranging from the sumptuous to the utilitarian, a casino, and even a small local airport. The name Dinard is said to come from the ancient Breton words *din* (hill) and *arz* (bear); the bear was sacred to the ancient Celts, and the animal was no doubt hunted – or worshipped – among the hills inland from the Côte d'Emeraude.

Until the 1850s, Dinard was just a small fishing village attached to Saint-Enogat, which now forms the western part of the resort. At about that time wealthy British visitors started spending their summers there in rented cottages. The holiday home built by a shadowy figure called Copinger, referred to usually as 'a rich American', is said to have been responsible for launching Dinard on its career as a resort. A descendant of Mr Copinger, Mrs Jenet Peers, has delved into his background, and kindly passed on to me the results of her researches. In spite of his American-sounding

name, James Erhart Copinger (1812–63) was a Frenchman; in 1845 he bought some land in Dinard and built a mansion on what must then have been an empty promontory, with magnificent views out to sea and across the Rance estuary. Called Le Bec de la Vallée, the gabled, gothic-looking house still exists, now turned into flats, in a street (Rue Coppinger, with two 'p's) that perpetuates its builder's name.

In the 1870s Henry Blackburn, a successful Victorian journalist, made several visits to Brittany and recorded his impressions of Dinard in his book *Breton Folk*. He found about 800 'houses and villas in pleasant gardens' let for the summer, and the casino was doing good business. The Côte d'Emeraude was the ideal place for a quiet bucket-and-spade seaside holiday.

> At Dinard you play at croquet on the sands; at St Briac you scramble over granite rocks, and fish in pools under their shadows; at St Jacut you wander over the sands with a shrimp-net, and in the evenings help the nuns to draw water from the well.

*Breton Folk* was published in 1880; but with a few minor changes of detail this passage could just as well be describing the 1990s.

From Dinard there is a fine view across the Rance to the granite walls of Saint-Malo, looming above the cross-Channel car ferries and the masts of hundreds of smaller craft. East of Dinard you complete the circuit back to Saint-Malo by way of the Usine Marémotrice, a tidal barrage across the mouth of the Rance, whose giant turbines produce electricity for the local grid. Before returning to Saint-Malo, it is worth spending some time in Saint-Servan, its southern offshoot. A resort in its own right, Saint-Servan has wide squares and gardens, and several beaches facing across to Dinard. Its small harbour is guarded by the Tour Solidor, a massive tower built in the 1380s probably on Roman foundations; it is now a museum of the Cap-Horniers, the graceful sailing clippers that once plied the trade routes round Cape Horn.

*The fourteenth-century Tour Solidor guards the little harbour of Saint-Servan, now a suburb of Saint-Malo. Inside the tower is a museum devoted to the Cape Horn sailing clippers.*

41

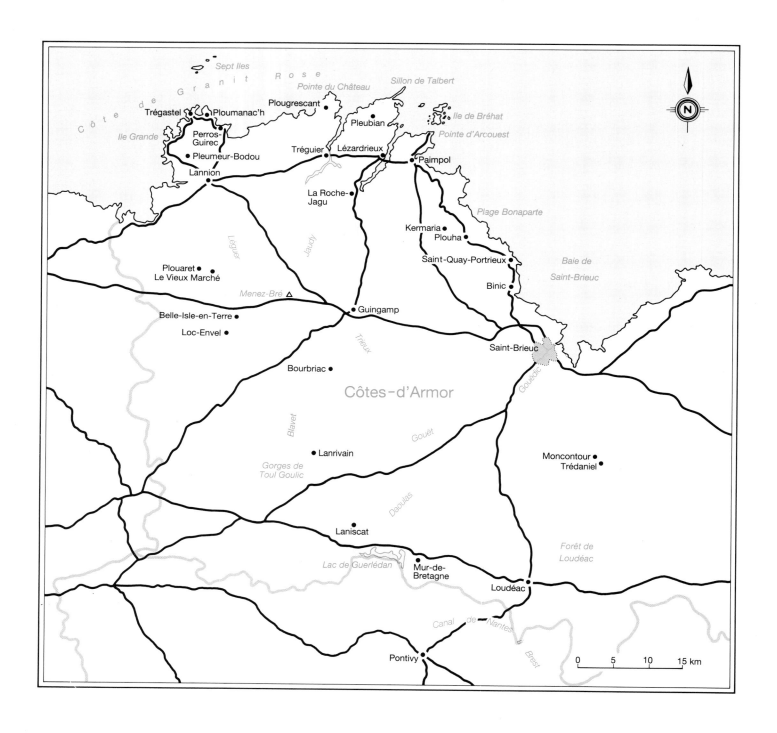

# 2
# The Côte de Granit Rose

*Guingamp – Saint-Brieuc – Paimpol – Ile de Bréhat*

*Perros-Guirec – Lannion*

Guingamp is a typical Breton provincial town, with a medieval nucleus of gabled granite houses engulfed in a sea of industrial estates and housing developments. Standing at the hub of a network of roads, it has been an important commercial centre since the Middle Ages, and still breathes an atmosphere of quiet prosperity. Its name goes back to the Dark Ages, when the Bretons built a *gwen camp* ('white camp', or possibly 'blessed camp') above the River Trieux, as a refuge from the Norse longships ravaging their coast. It is the easternmost town to be Breton in every sense of the word, as it stands on what was once the dividing line between the Breton-speaking (*bretonnant*) and the French-speaking (*francisant*) halves of Brittany.

Though its centre does not have the immediate impact of many ancient Breton towns, it has two remarkable architectural treasures – a partly renaissance church of near-cathedral size and a totally renaissance fountain, within a couple of minutes' walk of each other in the pedestrianized part of the town. Start your exploration in the Place du Centre. The fountain, at its lower end, is known as La Plomée, either from the lead used in its construction, or from

the Breton *poull-men* ('basin of stone'). A riot of nymphs, dolphins and griffins rises on three basins of diminishing size, with water splashing down from one to the other.

A short way up Rue Notre Dame, the twin porches of Guingamp's huge and extraordinary church open directly on to the street. Dedicated to Our Lady of True Succour (Notre Dame de Bon Secours or, in Breton, Itron Varia Gwir Zikour), it combines gothic and renaissance in a most original way. The two building styles do more than co-exist, as the renaissance has been grafted on to the gothic, and interpenetrates it both outside and inside. The old buildings of the town press so close upon the church that it is hard to take in as a whole; but the difference between the two epochs is summed up by the two west towers.

The north-west tower (Tour de l'Horloge) is thirteenth-century gothic, with a pyramidal roof capped by a little bell turret; while the south-west tower – known for some reason as the Tour Plate, though it is far from flat – is a massively buttressed sixteenth-century structure, with a Latin inscription proclaiming it 'a tower of strength against the enemy'. A battery of stone cannon jutting from the parapet give

*Above a door in the old part of Guingamp, an elaborate renaissance carving features the scallop shell worn by pilgrims to St James's shrine at Santiago de Compostela, in north-west Spain.*

teeth to the proclamation. Major reconstruction became necessary after most of the medieval south-west tower collapsed in 1535, leaving – so says a stone inscription – *la grande ruisne, piteuse à voir* ('a great ruin, pitiful to behold'). The citizens of Guingamp put the rebuilding out to competition. The winning architect was Jean le Moal, a young enthusiast for the new renaissance style, which was revolutionary in Brittany at that time; and it says much for the go-ahead outlook of sixteenth-century Guingamp that he was given a free hand. The street that leads round behind the church is named after him.

Once inside, you are immediately struck by the gothic-renaissance contrast. Most of the tall, narrow interior is typically gothic, with pointed windows, and delicate internal flying buttresses supporting the slender columns of the choir. But in his spectacular rebuilding of the whole south-west corner Le Moal made no attempt to harmonize his work with the older style. The triforium gallery was recast in the most fanciful way. It consists of a double arcade surmounted by S-shaped scrolling, and a strange recessed gangway above, with uprights that look like stone chair-legs. Each bay of the arcade is topped by a scallop shell below the gothic vault. Such scallops are carved all over the church inside and out; traditionally associated with St James, they suggest that Notre Dame was a staging-post on the pilgrim route to his shrine at Santiago de Compostela in north-west Spain – a suggestion made more probable by the brightly painted statue of the saint, with a scallop shell in his hat, which stands below the organ gallery.

During the French Revolution Notre Dame suffered the usual indignities: the porch was turned into a guardroom, the sacristy into a prison, the tower into a powder-magazine, and the body of the church into a hay-store. Damage caused by the Revolutionaries was not made good until the mid nineteenth century. Further damage occurred towards the end of World War II, when the tall spire on the central tower was destroyed by an American shell during the liberation of Guingamp in 1944. It was rebuilt in 1955.

In a church full of unusual features, perhaps the most unusual is the north-west porch, dedicated to Notre Dame. Rows of candles burn before a Black Madonna, set in a wall-niche; while the floor is laid out with a stone labyrinth, leading the pilgrim to the words AVE MARIA at its centre. This Madonna is the focal point of the *pardon* held in Guingamp on the first Saturday in July, decorous enough today, though a century and a half ago it was as much pagan as Christian. Such *pardons* are held in every Breton town,

*The renaissance fountain of La Plomée, decorated with nymphs, dolphins and griffins, stands in the heart of old Guingamp. Behind is the medieval north-west tower of the church of Notre Dame de Bon Secours.*

and most villages, each year. Beginning in the Middle Ages as penitential processions through the streets of the town behind the relics of the local saint, they evolved into full-scale religious festivals, sometimes lasting for days, and are now largely an excuse for local merrymaking – though the religious undercurrent is still present, and the priest often plays a major part.

The Breton author Emile Souvestre, writing about the Guingamp *pardon* in the 1830s, described the revelry after the procession was over:

> Cries of joy, shouted names, bursts of laughter succeed the contemplative dignity of the nocturnal procession. The crowd of penitents gather in the square, where they all have to sleep higgledy-piggledy on the bare ground. So the holy ceremony in honour of the Immaculate Virgin ends more often than not in an orgy. The girls and boys meet and mingle, take one another's arms, excite one another, chase one another through the dark streets; and the next day, when the sun rises, many girls rejoin their mothers with red faces and downcast eyes, and one sin more to confess to the parish priest.

After looking inside the church, go round to the south side to see its less public aspect, away from the crowds in the main street. Here the outer façade of Le Moal's organ loft, with its gable and square mullioned windows, looks more like a château than a church.

Guingamp is the only town I have come across, in Brittany or anywhere else, where a bank is also an art gallery. The Crédit Mutuel, in Rue Notre Dame, is more like a smart private house than a bank; the large rooms on its upper floor show paintings by local artists, in an imaginative collaboration between the worlds of culture and commerce. At the top of the town Rue Notre Dame leads into a broad square (Place de Verdun), dominated by the bland seventeenth-century façade of the former hospital (Hôtel Dieu), now the Mairie. What is left of Guingamp's medieval castle is just off the square, above the river. A few walls survive of the fifteenth-century château, demolished in 1626 on the orders of Cardinal Richelieu.

Guingamp was the birthplace in 1864 of the composer Guy Ropartz, one of Brittany's few academic composers. A pupil of Massenet and César Franck, he wrote four symphonies, chamber music, operas and incidental music for the stage, church works and songs, much of it based on Breton folksong. He taught for many years in Nancy and Strasbourg, and died aged over 90 in 1955. With the tremendous enthusiasm for traditional music found today throughout Brittany, there should surely be at least a small place at the many annual festivals for the music of Ropartz and other 'serious' Breton composers.

From Guingamp, no fewer than nine main routes radiate to every part of the Côtes-d'Armor *département*. Take the comparatively minor D8 south into some of Brittany's wildest and most unspoilt countryside. Bourbriac, the first place of any consequence, has a majestic church out of all proportion to the size of the village. It gets its name from St Briac, patron saint of the region, who was born in Ireland in the sixth century and crossed to Brittany, by way of Wales, as a disciple of St Tugdual. The church took eight centuries from foundation to completion: the crypt, supported on sturdy romanesque pillars, dates from the eleventh century, while the tall spire dates from the end of the nineteenth. St Briac died about 570; his relics were much visited by sufferers from mental disorders, and during the Middle Ages Bourbriac became a place of pilgrimage. Epileptics were taken down to the crypt, where they could follow the service without disturbing the congregation overhead.

Just before Lanrivain, you pass the roadside chapel of Notre Dame du Guiaudet, built at the end of the seventeenth century, after a local peasant discovered a miracle-working statue of the Virgin. Apart from the statue, the chapel has an electric carillon which plays Breton folk tunes on its sixteen bells, and a reredos carved with the Virgin lying down beside the infant Christ, rare in Breton iconography.

---

*The seventeenth-century chapel of Sainte-Suzanne, Mur-de-Bretagne, was a favourite subject of the nineteenth-century artist Camille Corot.*

At Lanrivain, off the main road, you are back in the ancient world of Breton religion. The fifteenth-century ossuary beside the church is piled with skulls, thigh-bones and varied skeletal fragments, unlike the ossuaries on the usual tourist track, which have been emptied of their *memento mori* contents, and give no hint of their charnel-house origins. Among the carvings on the ancient calvary (sculptured crucifixion group) is a sombrely impressive entombment. Such calvaries are found all over Brittany; they range from simple wayside stone crucifixes where the traveller could offer up a prayer for a successful journey, to elaborate constructions covered with dozens of lifelike figures from the Passion story.

South of Lanrivain, back roads lead to one of Brittany's most dramatic natural features. The Toul Goulic gorge is a deep and wildly romantic valley, cut by the fast-flowing River Blavet. Lined with trees whose roots grip the rocks on either side, its floor is a wilderness of giant rounded boulders, some as big as cottages and many of them covered with a skin of soft green moss. At the upper end of the gorge the river disappears below the surface and runs for a half a kilometre or so beneath the boulders, rumbling gently to itself with a noise like a distant underground train. Primitive man must surely have lived in the overhang of some of the Toul Goulic's monster stones, and worshipped its roaring subterranean god.

South-east of here, the River Daoulas has carved itself an equally impressive gorge, where the picturesque D44 twists for a few kilometres from the village of Laniscat down to the N164, with the river on one side and high walls of shattered rock on the other. On a fine summer's day, when the sun shines on hillsides bright with broom and gorse among the heather, this gorge is cheerful enough; but on an overcast day it can seem gloomy and menacing.

Brittany is not particularly rich in abbey ruins, and most of them have a rather forlorn look. This is certainly the case at Notre Dame de Bon Repos, at the southern end of the Daoulas gorge. The minor monastic buildings have been turned into a restaurant-cum-hotel, while what remains of the medieval church is buried under ivy and appears to be in a dangerously crumbling condition. Twelve Cistercian monks came to this beautiful site beside the Blavet in 1184, from Savigny in Normandy, at the instigation of Vicomte Alain de Rohan. He was inspired to choose the spot by the Virgin, who recommended it for his soul's 'good repose'. Though the abbey ruins may be disappointing, Bon Repos has a splendid medieval bridge.

Downstream from Bon Repos, the Blavet has been dammed to form the sinuous windings of the Lac de Guerlédan, now thoroughly naturalized into the landscape after more than sixty years of existence. It is well worth taking one of the little roads that lead down to the lake, as in summer it is a magical scene of water and woodland, with yachts and windsurfers skittering across its surface.

Guerlédan's hydro-electric dam must be a constant worry to the people of Mur-de-Bretagne, who live directly below it. Why their unwarlike village should be called 'Wall of Brittany' is something of a mystery. It has a nineteenth-century church, and a pretty though dilapidated seventeenth-century chapel dedicated to St Suzanne. Standing on a stretch of grass surrounded by oak trees, the chapel was a favourite subject of the artist Camille Corot (1796–1875).

From Mur-de-Bretagne, drive south to Pontivy, as near the geographical centre of Brittany as makes no difference. Pontivy stands on the Blavet, which by this stage in its career has become a considerable river, wide enough to form part of the Nantes–Brest Canal. Napoleon appreciated Pontivy's strategic position and destined it for great things, renaming it Napoléonville – the name died with his exile, but reappeared briefly under the Second Empire in the nineteenth century.

Pontivy is said to have been founded some time before 700 by a Welsh monk, Ivy or Yvi, who built the first bridge across the river, hence its name. Two or

*Swollen by spring rains, the River Daoulas tumbles over the boulders of the Gorges du Daoulas in one of the wildest parts of central Brittany.*

three streets of half-timbered buildings remain from the medieval town which grew up around the castle. Built at the end of the fifteenth century by Vicomte Jean de Rohan, the present castle stands on the site of an eleventh-century fortification, destroyed by the English in 1342. Its massively squat walls, terminating in circular towers, dominate the town; inside are some magnificent sixteenth-century stone fireplaces, carved with coats-of-arms and heraldic beasts. The complex timbers of the conical tower roofs are well worth studying, as they are masterpieces of the joiner's art. During the summer the great gallery between the towers is used for offbeat exhibitions; the theme of a recent one was witchcraft, alchemy and associated arts, both black and white. The lower storey of the north tower contains a small collection of obsolete printing-presses.

From Pontivy, head north-east to Loudéac, an unmemorable town famous in earlier centuries for growing flax, and now a centre for making *charcuterie* and animal feeds. The Forêt de Loudéac, north-east of the town, was once part of the Forêt de Brocéliande which covered the whole of central Brittany. Wolves are said to have been shot here as recently as the nineteenth century.

North of Loudéac, branch right on the D768 to Moncontour, a cosily compact little town, still largely medieval, built round a neat central square of granite houses. It stands on a spur of land where two river valleys meet, and during the constant wars of the Middle Ages was an important strategic town, besieged on three separate occasions. A good deal of the ramparts survives, together with several of the town gates. The sixteenth-century church, dedicated to St Mathurin, has six superb stained-glass windows on biblical themes, dating from around 1500.

Devotees of unusual saints, or hypochondriacs, should hunt out the chapel of Notre Dame du Haut,

*The corner turret and gables of the massive château at Pontivy, built in the fifteenth century on earlier foundations.*

*A statue of St Yvertin in the chapel of Notre Dame du Haut, near Moncontour. One of Brittany's 'Seven Healing Saints', Yvertin (here wrongly inscribed as 'Livertin') is believed to cure persistent headaches.*

which stands on a grassy knoll outside the village of Trédaniel just east of Moncontour. Inside the austere little seventeenth-century chapel stands a row of brightly painted statues of Brittany's Sept Saints Guérisseurs ('Seven Healing Saints'). There is hardly an illness that does not come into the domain of one or other of them. St Yvertin holds his head, to show that he is concerned with migraines. St Houarniaule (or Hervé) cures irrational fears; he holds a wolf on the end of a leash, as in former times such fears were supposed to be caused by catching sight of a *loup-garou*, or werewolf. St Hubert, with billhook, cures wounds; St Méen wards off madness; St Lubin takes care of eye disorders and rheumatism; while St Mamert holds open his intestines, to show that he is concerned with

51

digestive complaints. The only woman in the group, St Eugénie, ensures an easy delivery in childbirth.

Cynics may smile at the naivety of the concept; yet the number of modern votive plaques with *merci* engraved on them show that, to the faithful at least, the Healing Saints are still as effective as any doctor. A *pardon* is held here each year on August 15.

The chapel owes its existence, and its dedication to the Virgin, to yet another miracle. Some time during the fifteenth century a traveller was set upon by brigands, who robbed him and prepared to hang him from an oak tree. Looking up into the tree, he was amazed to see a statue of the Virgin on one of its branches. He made a vow that if she saved him, he would take the statue, run as far as he could with it, and build a chapel for it at the spot where he collapsed with exhaustion. The Virgin approved; an angel appeared and put the brigands to flight; the traveller ran with the statue as far as the grassy knoll above Trédaniel; and the chapel was duly built. The story is depicted on one of the stained-glass windows.

Back in Moncontour, make for Saint-Brieuc along the D1. The capital of the Côtes-d'Armor *département*, and an expanding and busy commercial and industrial centre, Saint-Brieuc is not as picturesque as many of Brittany's more historic towns. However, it is not a city to be rushed through, as its old centre is well worth exploring. It stands on a magnificent site between two rivers, the Gouédic on the east and the Gouët on the west, some 3 kilometres from the sea; and owes much of its drama, as well as its traffic problems, to its hilly situation.

Saint-Brieuc's foundation dates back to the late sixth century, when the Welsh monk Brioc or Brieuc sailed across the Channel, landed in Saint-Brieuc Bay, and set up a monastic community somewhere near the present Rue de la Fontaine Saint-Brieuc. A town grew

*A modern carving in Saint-Brieuc Cathedral, one of the Stations of the Cross by Saupique.*

up round the monastery, and during the tenth century its inhabitants fought constant battles with the invading Normans.

The frowning medieval St Stephen's Cathedral was largely built in the early thirteenth century by Guillaume Pinchon, a 'battling bishop' who fought the duke of Brittany and was canonized soon after his death in 1234. It stands on marshy ground, supported on piles driven into the soil, and its twin towers, battlemented and pierced with arrow slits, give it the appearance of a fortress rather than a church. Much of it was destroyed by fire in 1353, and rebuilt by the duke of Brittany of the day. The nave, rebuilt in the eighteenth century, was used during the Revolution as stabling for horses. The cathedral is worth going into for the tomb of St Guillaume in the south aisle, a splendid fifteenth-century rose window in the south transept, and modern stations of the Cross.

*A half-timbered house in a street near the thirteenth-century cathedral of Saint-Brieuc, a mainly modern city with a medieval heart.*

Saint-Brieuc has some fine public gardens, notably the Grandes Promenades high above the Gouëdic valley, where you can stroll along wide paths between sweeping flower-beds. Among the statues is a bust of the novelist and playwright Auguste Villiers de l'Isle-Adam, who was born in Saint-Brieuc in 1838. A devout Catholic, he was a pioneer of the Symbolist movement, writing short stories in the manner of Edgar Allan Poe. On the north side of the town is Saint-Brieuc's harbour, the Port du Légué, where St Brioc is said to have landed. Sheltered by the deep valley of the Gouët, it can take ships of 1500 tonnes and more, and is a centre for sea-fishing of all sorts.

The road to Paimpol up the west side of the Baie de Saint-Brieuc (D786) bypasses dozens of small bays and inlets, many of them with tiny seaside resorts reached down narrow lanes. Two resorts have reached substantial size, and are now largely given over to marinas and moorings for small craft: Binic, once home to a fishing fleet that sailed as far as Iceland to fish for cod; and Saint-Quay-Portrieux, which has four good beaches, and is sophisticated enough to boast a casino.

Not surprisingly, many of the saints who sailed across from England in the early days of Breton Christianity are said to have made their landfall on this accessible coast; while World War II saw traffic in the other direction, with Allied aircrew, shot down over occupied France, smuggled out of the creeks under the noses of the Germans. This traffic is commemorated by a monument beside the Plage Bonaparte – a forbiddingly stony beach, reached down a cul-de-sac from the D786 2 kilometres north of the small town of Plouha.

It requires some effort of the imagination to visualize the beach in its wartime loneliness, as there is now a large car-park behind it and a tunnel has been burrowed through the rock to give easy access to the foreshore. An inscription at the mouth of the tunnel describes how, between January and August 1944, 135 Allied airmen 'embarked in secret for England on dark nights'. The rescue operation was given the code name Bonaparte – hence the present name for the beach, formerly known as the Anse Cochat (Cochat Cove). The message that a lift-off would be taking place was transmitted by the BBC through the code sentence *Bonjour à tous dans la maison d'Alphonse*, referring to a small cottage on the clifftop; while cancellation of a mission was notified by *Denise, ta soeur est morte*.

The French writer Rémy (Gilbert Renault), who was himself a resistance fighter elsewhere in France, has left an account of the mingled boredom and excitement of such rescue operations in his book *La Maison d'Alphonse*. The airmen would be taken in twos and threes from the safe houses where they were sheltered to the rendezvous in the Maison d'Alphonse. From there they would be guided through the minefield at the top of the cliff and down the steep path to the beach, to wait for the dinghies to take them off. The Plage Bonaparte was not a safe place from which to send a signal to the British corvette carrying out the operation, as the jutting Pointe de la Tour a little to the north was the site of a German outpost. So the Resistance team signalled that they were ready by means of a blue lamp shining steadily in a cardboard tube, operating from inside a cave out of view of the Germans. Simultaneously a man hidden half-way up the cliff flashed the letters B or H in Morse code out to sea. The operation went so smoothly that the British nicknamed it the 'Channel bus service'.

About 3 kilometres inland from Plouha, the small chapel of Kermaria-an-Iskuit ('House of Mary the Healer') is full of unexpected treasures. Above the porch is the courtroom used for trials in the days of feudal justice, with the balcony from which sentences were pronounced. The porch contains painted statues of the apostles, while inside the chapel are further statues, among them a carving of the Virgin breast-feeding her child and wearing sabots, which poke out from the hem of her dress. Most astonishing of all are the frescoes over the arcades. Painted in about 1500, they show a Dance of Death containing 47 characters,

*Looking south from the Plage Bonaparte, the stony beach from which during World War II dozens of shot-down Allied aircrew were smuggled back to England.*

in which skeletons and corpses alternate with the living of all classes and trades, from king to ploughman, from money-lender to monk.

Back on the D786, just south of Paimpol, are the ruins of Beauport Abbey, surrounded by trees above Paimpol Bay. It was founded in 1202 for monks of the Premonstratensian order, and remained an abbey until the Revolution, when it was turned into a gunpowder factory. Most of the surviving ruins date from the thirteenth century, including part of the transept and the choir, and the enormous refectory, which opens on to the Channel, and proves that medieval monks had a good eye for a view.

Like Binic down the coast, Paimpol was once a centre of the Icelandic cod-fishing industry, with a fleet of over eighty schooners that made the annual journey to those distant northern seas. Today the harbour is packed with small pleasure craft, though there are still a few workaday offshore fishing boats among the sleek white-painted yachts. Paimpol keeps its old memories alive in the Musée de la Mer, which covers local maritime history and the evolution of the fishing industry, with plenty of charts, ship models and old photographs. The port was put on the literary map by Pierre Loti, whose novel *Pêcheur d'Islande* ('The Iceland Fisherman'), published in 1886, brought the harsh realities of the cod-fisherman's life before a wide readership. Paimpol's seafaring tradition is kept up by a training school for officers of the merchant navy, the oldest such school in France.

From Paimpol, continue north until the road ends at the Pointe d'Arcouest, looking across a 4-kilometre channel to the idyllic Ile de Bréhat. Ten minutes away by boat, Bréhat is a traffic-free – and hence pollution-free – haven of plant and bird life, with an almost Mediterranean profusion of trees and shrubs, among them mimosa, figs and oleanders. The best way to enjoy it is to hire a bicycle when you get to the island,

*A secluded nineteenth-century villa near Paimpol reflected in its lake.*

and potter gently along its lanes. Bréhat is really two islands linked by an isthmus, with a small township, called simply Le Bourg, in its southern half. The northern coast forms a savage contrast with the gentle interior; made up of a chaotic jumble of the pink rocks from which this stretch of the Breton coast takes its name (Côte de Granit Rose), it is best seen from off shore, on one of the round-the-island boat trips that run throughout the summer.

During the fifth and sixth centuries, one of Bréhat's tiny offshore islets, Lavrec or Lavret, was the site of a famous school founded by St Budoc, at which future missionary-saints were trained for their proselytizing work. The foundations of their round beehive cells are still said to exist. In the Middle Ages Bréhat was famous for the adventurousness of its fishermen, who were sailing to the Newfoundland and Labrador fishing-banks long before Columbus 'discovered' America. Indeed, according to one story Columbus first heard about the New World from a Bréhat corsair called Coätenlen, whom he met at Lisbon in 1484, eight years before his epic voyage of discovery.

Return to Paimpol, and drive west along the D786 towards Tréguier. Across the Lézardrieux bridge, which gives sweeping views up and down the Trieux river, turn left along the D787 to the château of La Roche-Jagu, 10 kilometres upstream. The castle stands on a commanding site at the top of a tree-covered slope, on the steep left bank of the Trieux. Built in the fifteenth century, its fortified towers form part of the main building, which stands on the site of two earlier strongholds. It was restored in the 1970s and has been turned into a cultural centre, where art exhibitions, concerts and conferences are held in the summer.

Back in Lézardrieux, head north up the D20 to the tip of the Pleubian peninsula, which separates the estuaries of the Trieux and the Jaudy. It fades away at one of Brittany's oddest natural formations, the Sillon de Talbert – a narrow shingle spit, hardly more than 30m wide but extending 3 kilometres out to sea. Covered in sea-holly and other marine plants, it protects the Trieux estuary from the full force of the north-west gales. It has commercial value, as the local

*The fifteenth-century château of La Roche-Jagu, which stands on a commanding site overlooking the River Trieux, is now a cultural centre for the region.*

farmers collect the seaweed (*goémon*) and rot it down to use on their land. During World War II the Germans removed so much shingle and sand to build their coastal fortifications that the Sillon's ecology was almost destroyed. Today it is rigorously protected.

From the Sillon the D20 continues round the peninsula, through Pleubian village to Tréguier on the far side of the Jaudy. Tréguier is a fine old town, which would surely be as well known as Dinan if it were more accessible. As at Dinan, streets of ancient houses rise steeply from a boat-lined river bank towards the town centre. The town is dominated by the tall stone spire of the cathedral, pierced with holes of all shapes and sizes to lessen the force of the wind sweeping in from the sea to the north. Dedicated to St Tugdual, one of the 'Seven Founding Saints' and first bishop of Tréguier in

the sixth century, it is one of the most striking churches in Brittany. It is of unusual design, with three towers, one over the crossing, and one over each transept (the spire is above the south transept, which is also the main entrance).

Most of the cathedral dates from the thirteenth to fifteenth centuries, though the northern tower, called for some reason the 'Tour Hastings', is romanesque of the tenth or eleventh century. The interior is a harmonious blend of romanesque and gothic. The north transept's round arches have capitals decorated with interlaced patterns and naive human figures, while the vaulting of the gracefully arcaded choir is decorated with fifteenth-century paintings of angels holding scrolls. The choir contains a most unusual series of 46 renaissance choir stalls, carved with wild men and other fanciful motifs. Among the many statues is a powerful thirteenth-century wooden statue of Christ, kept in one of the side chapels in the apse. But the most significant carving, from the historical if not from the artistic viewpoint, is the triple wooden statue in the south transept, showing St Yves – Tréguier's home-grown saint and the patron of the world's lawyers – between a rich man and a poor man, in allusion to the most famous of his Solomon-like judgments.

Yves Hélory was born in 1253 in a manor-house at Minihy, on the outskirts of Tréguier. For ten years or so, from the age of 14, he studied law and theology at Paris University and elsewhere, finally entering the priesthood as an ecclesiastical lawyer. He spent nearly all his working life in Tréguier, where he was renowned for helping poor clients who could not afford legal fees. The legendary judgment shown in the Tréguier carving – and in every other portrayal of St Yves up and down Brittany – runs as follows. A rich

*The architectural complexity of Tréguier cathedral is well shown in this view from the cloister on the north side. The spire is pierced with holes to lessen the force of the wind.*

man had sued a poor man, on the grounds that the latter only kept body and soul together by the smells of cooking wafting out of the rich man's kitchen. So Yves borrowed a coin, struck it and made it ring in the rich man's ear, giving as his judgment that the sound of the coin would pay for the smell of the food.

As a parish priest, Yves worked tirelessly among the poor of Tréguier, building a hostel for paupers and looking after local orphans. His asceticism was proverbial: he always wore a hair shirt, and soaked his outer tunic in water to increase his discomfort; he lived mainly on bread and vegetable soup; and he spent most of the night in prayer and meditation, sleeping for a short time before dawn on a clay bed with straw spread over it. He died in 1303 aged only 49, worn out by hard work and self-imposed privations. His tomb in Tréguier cathedral soon became a place of pilgrimage, with miraculous rescues reported from people in danger who had invoked his name. He was canonized in 1347. Soon after his death his extraordinary honesty was made the subject of a Latin jingle:

*Sanctus Yvo erat Brito,*
*Advocatus et non latro,*
*Res miranda populo.*

*(St Yves was a Breton,*
*A lawyer and not a crook,*
*A matter of wonder to the people.)*

– a rhyme to be taken to heart by the throng of lawyers who gather in Tréguier every year for St Yves's great *pardon* on May 19, the anniversary of his death and canonization. A solemn procession from his tomb in the cathedral to his birthplace at Minihy follows the saint's skull in its jewelled casket.

Tréguier's other famous son, Ernest Renan, whose bulky statue sits slumped in the tree-lined square in front of the cathedral, was right at the opposite end of the religious spectrum. Born in 1823, he scandalized orthodox Roman Catholicism with his *Vie de Jésus*, published in 1863, in which he insisted that Christ was a man like any other – an 'incomparable man', but human nonetheless. His birthplace, a solid timber-framed house just off the square, is now a museum, full of portraits and maps of his extensive journeys. Ironically, Renan the doubter actually visited the Holy Land, whereas St Yves the believer hardly set foot outside his native parish.

From Tréguier, take the D8 north to Plougrescant. The chapel of Saint-Gonéry, in the centre of the village, has one of the oddest features of any building in Brittany – an almost corkscrew-like spire. It took this shape when the original framework decayed, allowing the lead roof covering to twist as it settled. When the framework was rebuilt the locals were so attached to the spire's strange appearance that they insisted it should be preserved. Inside, the wooden roof of the nave is painted with a marvellous series of naive biblical scenes, curiously byzantine-looking, though they date from the sixteenth century. A few years ago they were suffering badly from the effects of time and neglect; but they have been recently restored. On one typical panel Adam and Eve sit guiltily terrified, clad from head to foot in tiny leaves. Below them is a Last Supper, with Judas stealing away from the table at the promptings of a horned devil. On the floor of the chapel is a stone sarcophagus, in which – so visitors are assured – St Gonéry rowed himself across from Britain in the sixth century.

Beyond Plougrescant, lanes lead down to the Pointe du Château, where black outcrops jut like rotting fangs above the seaweed-covered foreshore. Just south-west of the Pointe is one of Brittany's most extraordinary sights, a cottage sandwiched between giant boulders, with the sea behind, and in front a limpid lagoon.

Returning to Tréguier, continue west for 5 kilometres along the D786, then turn right for Perros-Guirec along the D6. Perros-Guirec is the main resort of the Côtes-d'Armor, built around a headland, and merging westwards into the lesser resorts of Ploumanac'h and Trégastel. It has plenty of hotels, a splendid north-facing beach (the Plage de Trestraou), a casino, and a 'Thalassotherapy' or sea-cure centre, where those in search of health can be bombarded by high-pressure water jets, lie in a poultice of muddy seaweed, or submit to an auto-suggestion anti-smoking cure. Its double-barreled name comes from the Breton Penroz, which may mean either 'Top of the Hill' or 'Pink Headland', combined with the name of yet another obscure Celtic saint, Guirec, who like St Gonéry is said to have sailed across the Channel in a stone trough. A possible explanation for the popularity of this unlikely mode of transport in folklore is that troughs, or sarcophagi, were used as ballast on Celtic ships coming from Cornwall.

Bird-lovers should take the three-hour boat-trip from Perros-Guirec to the Sept Iles, which lie 5 kilometres offshore. These small islands are protected as one of France's main sea-bird sanctuaries, set up as long ago as 1912 by the Ligue pour la Protection des Oiseaux (LPO), after the birds had been hunted almost to extinction. All round the islands puffins skim over the waves like small clockwork toys, cormorants sit on the rocks or dive sinuously after fish, and gulls wheel screaming overhead, or perch awkwardly on narrow ledges. The boat lands you on the Ile aux Moines, where you can climb the lighthouse to see the view, and admire the precision of the lamp, which floats on mercury and is visible 35 kilometres out to sea.

Between Perros-Guirec and Trégastel you pass the beautiful fifteenth-century chapel of Notre Dame de la Clarté; built of the local glowing pink granite, it is one of the architectural jewels of the Tréguier region. An inscription dates its foundation to 1455, though it was still not finished thirty years later; the tower and spire were added in the sixteenth century. Over the main entrance porch is a time-worn granite statue of the Virgin and Child, and inside the chapel are several rustically carved wooden saints, among them St Nicholas, St Sebastian, and St Fiacre, patron saint of gardeners, with his iron-shod spade.

The chapel is said to have been built by a Breton fleet-commander, who was caught in a fog off the Sept Iles, and vowed to the Virgin that he would build a chapel in her honour if he came safe ashore. At that moment the fog lifted, giving a clear view (*clarté*) of the coast, and he was saved. Towards the end of World War II fog reappeared in the history of La Clarté, this time as its saviour. A German battalion was dug in on a

*The corkscrew spire of the little chapel of Saint-Gonéry, in Plougrescant. The chapel's interior is painted with naive biblical scenes.*

nearby hill, with their guns trained on Perros-Guirec, while American Flying Fortresses soared overhead, hoping to bomb them out of existence. On three successive days a blanket of fog rolled in from the sea, preventing combat; the war moved on, and the town and the chapel survived.

Nearby Ploumanac'h is a little resort in two sections, divided by a headland. If you go there in summer, when it is liable to be packed, leave your car above it and walk down to the village. Its main beach, named after St Guirec, is unusual in having a tiny oratory in the middle, consisting of a stone canopy sheltering a granite statue of the saint. The original wooden effigy suffered greatly in the past from having pins stuck in it by girls wanting husbands; it is now kept in the chapel above the beach.

Ploumanac'h owes its fame to the extraordinary pink granite boulders above the tideline, worn into fantastic animal and humanoid shapes by millennia of wind and sea spray. Some have a fancied resemblance to animals (tortoise, elephant, whale, ram), while others have been given whimsical names, such as Napoleon's Hat and the Death's Head. These rocks continue round to Trégastel, a larger resort than Ploumanac'h, with a choice of fine beaches.

South and west from Trégastel, the road (D788) skirts more good sandy beaches. After 6 kilometres or so, turn right to the Ile Grande, a windswept, rocky peninsula rather than a proper island. An ornithological centre has been set up here in recent years, where professional ornithologists carry out serious research, and the ordinary bird-watcher can learn about the bird life of the region from a permanent exhibition. An important part of the centre's work lies in the rehabilitation of birds affected by oil pollution – work given urgency by tanker disasters off the Breton coast, culminating in the break-up of the *Amoco Cadiz* off north Finistère in 1978.

The scrubby heathland inland from the Ile Grande is dominated by the huge white radome of France's first satellite telecommunications centre, set up at Pleumeur-Bodou in 1962. Near by a copper dome marks a planetarium, where you can watch 'the ballet of the planets and the stars', or find out all the latest astronomical discoveries from audio-visual displays. In contrast to this technological wizardry, in a combe below the radome archaeologists are gradually building a 'Gaulish Village', using as far as possible the techniques and materials current among the tribes of Brittany before the Romans came. When I saw it in 1988, they had built a huge timber-framed longhouse entirely without nails or metal fastenings of any sort,

*Slate-hung and half-timbered medieval façades in Lannion's Place du General Leclerc mark the town's ancient centre.*

*The tiny oratory of Saint-Guirec, on the beach at Ploumanac'h, shelters a statue of the saint. All around are the strange pinkish boulders of the Côte de Granit Rose, worn into fantastic shapes.*

and constructed open-air ovens and wash-places not so very different from those still to be seen here and there in the countryside. Young people from all over the world are encouraged to come and work here during the summer, making it a real international project.

Lannion, capital of the Côte de Granit Rose, is a short way inland from Pleumeur-Bodou. Since the opening of the telecommunications centre in the 1960s, it has changed from a sleepy market town to a flourishing centre of modern electronics. The River Léguer, which runs through the heart of the town, gives it an unusually spacious feeling. On the left bank are the buildings of a large eighteenth-century convent, while on the right the streets of old Lannion climb the steep hill above the river. The best of the ancient slate-hung houses are in the Place du Général Leclerc, the centre of

*The romanesque ambulatory of Brélévénez church, at the top of old Lannion, was built by the Knights Templar in the twelfth century.*

the town, reached from the river up the pedestrianized Rue des Augustins. At the far end is the large church of Saint-Jean de Baly, built mainly in the sixteenth century but never properly finished off, as its square tower is still incomplete.

Do not leave Lannion without climbing the 142 granite steps (or 140, or 144, count them yourself) to the splendid romanesque Brélévénez church, a rare example of twelfth-century architecture in Brittany, built by the Knights Templars. The tall tower dates from the fifteenth century, and the crypt contains an unusual eighteenth-century Holy Sepulchre. From the terrace on which the church stands there is a wide panorama over Lannion and the Léguer valley.

Heading south from Lannion, take the cross-country D11, branching left after 5 kilometres to the Château de Tonquédec, one of Brittany's most magnificent feudal ruins. Standing among trees above the Léguer valley, it was completed at the beginning of the fifteenth century and dismantled on the orders of Cardinal Richelieu in 1622. Its powerful curtain walls are guarded by turrets, and the central keep has walls 4m thick. The nearby Kerfons chapel, built in the fifteenth and sixteenth centuries, has a remarkable interior, with a fine decorated renaissance rood-screen, and windows containing sixteenth-century stained glass. Outside is an ancient calvary set among chestnut trees.

Back on the D11, turn left in Plouaret to Le Vieux Marché. A little north of the village is a pretty chapel in a grassy setting, with a unique dedication to Les Sept Saints. They are not, however, the usual Seven Founding Saints of Brittany, nor even the Seven Healing Saints found at Notre Dame du Haut, but the 'Seven Sleeping Saints of Ephesus'. These were young Christians from Ephesus in Asia Minor, who were walled up in a cave during the third century on the orders of the Roman emperor, for refusing to renounce their religion. Miraculously surviving for 200 years, they were released and returned to Ephesus with a hunger unsatisfied for two centuries. When they offered the fifth-century Ephesians third-century money in exchange for food, they were questioned, told their story, and not surprisingly were soon elevated to sainthood. In honour of their Near Eastern origin, Muslims as well as Christians take part in the *pardon* held at Les Sept Saints each July.

From Le Vieux Marché, head south along the D88, then east along the main road (N12), leaving it soon for Belle-Isle-en-Terre. This quiet little town, in a gentle countryside of lakes and rivers, was given its name by monks from the island of Belle-Ile (formerly known as Belle-Isle-en-Mer), who settled here in the Middle Ages. North of Belle-Isle, across the main road, is the hilltop chapel of Locmaria, which has a fine sixteenth-century rood-screen painted with the twelve apostles.

The village of Loc-Envel, 3 kilometres south of Belle-Isle, has a slightly older chapel, also with a fine rood-screen. Outside the village is a hilly tract of woodland with a strange Breton double name, half of it called

Coat-an-Noz ('Night Forest'), and half Coat-an-Hay ('Day Forest'). Similarly there are said to have been two St Envels, twin brothers who lived one in each forest. The Druids are known to have had special reverence for twins, so the legend may well go back to a pre-Christian past.

The only feature worth more than a glance on the road back to Guingamp is the hill known as Menez-Bré; though only just over 300m high, it is still the highest point in north Brittany, and dominates the surrounding countryside. (*Menez*, related to the Welsh *mynydd*, is simply the Breton for 'mountain'.) On its treeless summit, torn up in summer by motor-cycle scramblers, is a neat little chapel to St Hervé. In past centuries a funeral service known as the *Ofern Drantel* ('Thirtieth Mass', the last of the series of thirty masses held for the souls of the dead) was held at the hill-top chapel, to discourage the demons who crowded around trying to get their claws on the latest soul. The priest conducting the mass had to be barefoot and recite the service backwards, and afterwards had to give each demon a flax-seed, since, legend has it, 'devils never agree to leave empty-handed'.

*Carved figures on the sixteenth-century rood screen in the hilltop chapel of Locmaria, Belle-Isle-en-Terre.*

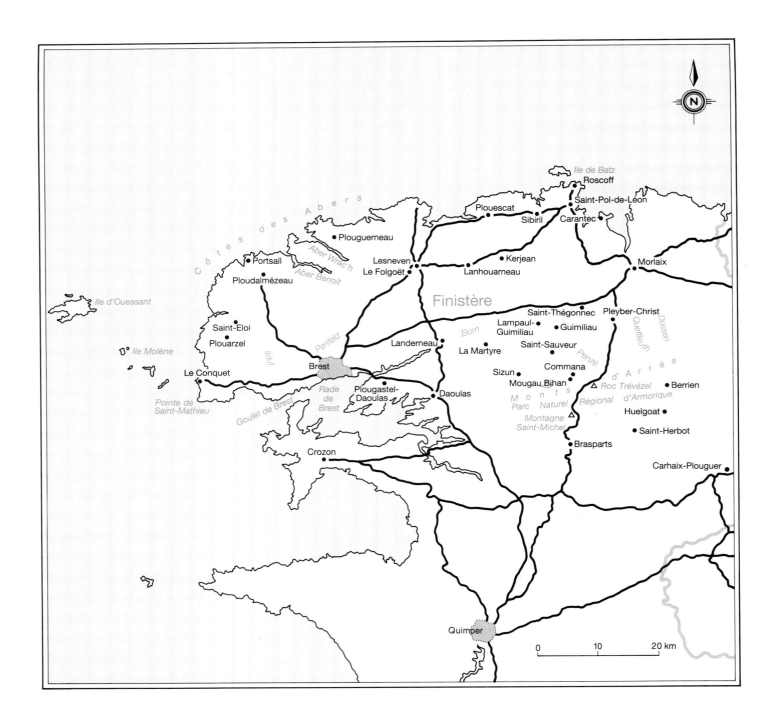

# 3
# North Finistère

*Morlaix – Huelgoat – Sizun – Landerneau – Brest*
*Ile d'Ouessant – Roscoff*

**M**orlaix is the chief town of north Finistère, built along the valley of the Dossen or Morlaix river, with enough half-timbered houses to remind visitors of its prosperity in the fifteenth and sixteenth centuries. But its chief landmark is the lordly arched viaduct built in the 1860s to carry the railway between Paris and Brest. Towering 58m high, it strides across the valley and effectively divides the town into two sections: inland the streets of old Morlaix, with narrow lanes rising steeply from the valley floor; and below it the river, lined with eighteenth-century quayside houses and now turned into a marina.

The town's Breton name is Montroulez; its French name is the basis of a pun in the Morlaix motto: *S'ils te mordent, mord-les* ('If they bite you, bite them back'). This dates back to an English raid on Morlaix in 1522, in reprisal for an attack on Bristol by Morlaix corsairs. The English troops found it undefended, as most of the inhabitants were at an out-of-town festival. They pillaged the houses and then proceeded to drink themselves senseless in the cellars; when the locals returned they found them helpless and massacred them, so that the town fountain is said to have run red with English blood. Besides the motto, the Morlaix coat of arms features the French leopard and the English lion, face to face in mutual hostility.

By this period Morlaix had become a leading port, reaching the height of its prosperity between the sixteenth and eighteenth centuries. It traded with Portugal, Spain and Holland, built ships, made sails and fine cloth, processed and sold tobacco, and produced ornate goldsmiths' work. It also bred generations of corsairs, of whom the most successful was Charles Cornic, born at Morlaix in 1731. If you park down by the harbour (the best place, in a town never designed for modern traffic) and walk towards the centre of Morlaix below the viaduct, you pass a bust of Cornic gazing towards the marina where his privateers once anchored.

Once through the viaduct, walk left up to the gabled Saint-Melaine church, which stands in the shadow of its mighty arches. The oldest church in Morlaix, it was built in Flamboyant gothic style at the end of the fifteenth century, on the site of a twelfth-century priory church, and celebrated its 500th anniversary in 1989. Outside, above the main porch, carved angels hold a worn scroll on which you can just make out the foundation date 1489, in a medieval spelling and script:

*L'An Mil Quatre Cents Quatre Vingnts Neuff.* St Melaine, its dedicatee, was a sixth-century bishop of Rennes. Inside, the wall-plates (*sablières*) below the roof-vault are carved and brightly painted, with all sorts of human and animal motifs.

From Saint-Melaine, walk up the steps of the steep and narrow Venelle aux Prêtres ('Priests' Lane'), between ancient granite-built houses; then through the upper arches of the viaduct – here within touching distance – to the tree-lined Esplanade du Calvaire, with views across the valley to the other side of the town. When the viaduct was built, the harbour came right to its base, covering the sites of today's public gardens and car-park, which are on reclaimed land. Towards the end of World War II Allied aircraft bombed the viaduct; they succeeded in damaging it severely, but in the process hit an infant school, killing a class of 39 children and their teacher.

A high-level path zigzags round to the Fontaine des Carmélites, one of Morlaix's prettiest corners. The spring, protected by twin stone arches, is just outside the gates of a convent, still occupied by Carmelite nuns. The small chapel behind it has a graceful rose window, now blocked up. When I went there, two locals passing the time of day told me that they never saw French people up there, only foreigners.

Several *venelles* lead back down to the lower levels of the town. Beside the wide Place des Jacobins, the Musée des Jacobins is housed in a white-painted medieval church, formerly the church of a Jacobin (Dominican) priory. Lit in part by a magnificent fifteenth-century rose window, the collections cover all aspects of life in north Finistère, formerly known as Léon, from archaeology to agriculture, and from shipbuilding to religious art. Near by, in the Place Allende (previously Place des Halles) and the pedestrianized Grand' Rue, are some of the best of the town's medieval merchants' houses, a number of them decorated with religious or grotesque carvings.

A Morlaix Dominican who left a great reputation behind him was Père Albert Le Grand, chronicler of Brittany's thousands of saints. Born towards the end of the sixteenth century, in 1636 he completed his *Vies des Saints de la Bretagne-Armorique*, the classic source-book on the byways of Breton faith. In his preface he wrote: 'I forbid absolutely that this book should be read by Atheists, by Freethinkers, by the Uncommitted, by Heretics, and by those conceited persons who calculate the power of God according to the measure of their ill-tuned brains'. After such a warning, it might be thought that Le Grand's *Lives* would consist of nothing but religious platitudes, but they are in fact highly readable. Sadly, he did not enjoy his success for very long, as he died early in the 1640s, after revising and adding to his *Lives*.

From Morlaix, take the D769 due south in the direction of Carhaix-Plouguer. This is one of Brittany's most delightful roads, running first along the wooded valley of the Queffleuth (one of the two streams that meet at Morlaix), then climbing to a breezy, open landscape of heath and gorse. As a further bonus, even in midsummer you will hardly meet another car, as the road does not really lead anywhere. In the pretty stone village of Berrien, turn off for Huelgoat. Berrien is on the northern boundary of the Parc Naturel Régional d'Armorique, which takes in the hills of central Finistère, with offshoots in the Crozon peninsula and the island of Ouessant (Ushant). France's regional nature parks consist of outstanding countryside, often under-developed by comparison with neighbouring areas, which require a watchful eye and helping hand if they are not to be prettified into tourist reserves, or degenerate into wilderness.

The country town of Huelgoat, with its wide tree-lined main street, is the Parc d'Armorique's small metropolis. It stands above a lake whose banks have been domesticated by a scattering of little white holiday homes. In past centuries it was a lead-mining centre, but is now completely rural; last time I was

*Yachts rest at anchor in the Morlaix marina. Behind are the classical blocks of the city's tobacco factory, founded in the eighteenth century when Morlaix was at the height of its prosperity.*

there a string of Brittany's powerful draught horses, the Trait Breton, was clopping sedately across the square among the traffic. Inside the sixteenth-century church is a statue of St Yves of Tréguier, portrayed as usual between a rich man and a poor man.

East of the town is one of the most picturesque small areas in Brittany – a jumble of boulders, fast-flowing streams and woodland, marked out with walks lasting anything from half an hour to three hours. The names give a good idea of the scenery: Chaos, Trembling Rock, Devil's Cave, Alley of the Clear Stream. A little to the north is the impressive Camp d'Artus, which has only a legendary connection with King Arthur. It is in fact a Gallo-Roman fortified site, probably from the first century.

Leave Huelgoat south along the D14, an up-and-down road which alternates wooded valleys with high heathland, giving distant views to the west of the Monts d'Arrée, Brittany's highest hills. Such views may not be there to enjoy much longer, as much of the bare countryside has been planted with young conifers; eventually they will turn the bare hills of Finistère into a miniature Black Forest, with no view except that of endless sombre pine trees.

The village of Saint-Herbot, 7 kilometres from Huelgoat, has an unusually large and elaborate sixteenth-century gothic chapel. Herbot is the patron saint of horned animals, and inside the chapel are two stone altars on which farmers leave tufts of hair from their cattle, to guarantee his favour in the coming year.

After another 13 kilometres, turn right on the D785 in the direction of Morlaix. The first village you come to, Brasparts, is on the southern edge of the Regional Nature Park; it has a superb parish close (*enclos paroissial*) dating from the sixteenth century. Such closes are unique to Finistère, and in their fully developed form consist of four basic elements: a parish

*A fearsome animal head grips a tiebeam below the painted vault of the church of St Melaine.*

*Behind the ornate lantern tower of the fifteenth-century church of St Melaine, a 19th-century railway viaduct strides high over Morlaix.*

church, a triumphal arch forming an impressive entry to the churchyard, an ossuary or mortuary chapel where the bones of the dead were stored, and a calvary, surmounted by a sculpted Crucifixion group, and often carved with scenes from the life of Christ. Built in the period 1450–1700, they were composite works of religious art by the finest Breton architects, sculptors, woodcarvers and painters of their day.

Though Brasparts has no triumphal arch, three of the main elements are present. The calvary has a tenderly sculptured *pietà* of three mourning figures holding the dead Christ; while the original function of the ossuary, now used in summer as a tourist information centre, is emphasized by a carving of the Ankou, the Bretons' skeletal personification of death. The church has a grandly pinnacled south porch, lined with statues of the apostles. It has been under

71

*A Stone Age construction in the hamlet of Mougau-Bihan, near Commana. This fine example of an* allée couverte *or passage grave was probably constructed about 2500* BC.

restoration since 1982, and work will probably not be completed until the mid 1990s.

North of Brasparts a tarmac track takes you up to the top of the Montagne Saint-Michel, at 380m almost the highest point in Brittany (the Roc Trévezel, a spiny ridge 10 kilometres to the north, is a few metres higher). At its summit is a chapel to St Michael, the patron saint of all such high places. Though empty and bare, it has at least been made structurally sound in the past few years; when I first saw it in the 1970s, the doors were banging in the wind, slates were missing from the roof, and the floor was a rubbish tip. On a clear day the view from the top is spectacular: north and south over rock and moorland, west towards the distant waters of the Rade de Brest, and east across marshland to a large reservoir, with the hulking blocks of the Brennilis atomic power station on its far side.

Continue north from the Montagne Saint-Michel, and turn off after 5 kilometres for the village of Commana. This has a fine example of a parish close in its complete form; but before making for it, hunt out the hamlet of Mougau Bihan, where one of Brittany's finest Stone Age survivals lurks on the outskirts. This *allée couverte*, which probably dates from about 2500 BC, consists of two lines of stone uprights with giant blocks laid across the top, forming a narrow corridor. Some of the stones are carved with symbolic designs, which are hard to make out, but have been interpreted as axes, spears and the breasts of a funeral goddess. When first constructed, the stones would have been covered with earth and turfed over, forming a huge funeral mound.

Commana's grey granite church is of a size and grandeur unexpected in so small a place; but it dates from a time when this part of Brittany was far more prosperous than it is today. Local landowners grew rich from the profits of flax and hemp, which were processed into cloth and traded all over Europe, or used at home to make sails for the French navy. The church's tall spire, built in the 1590s, is 57m high and one of the landmarks of the Monts d'Arrée. The south entrance porch is built in a rustic adaptation of renaissance style, with flanking columns and a broken pediment; in the uppermost niche is a statue of St Derrien, patron saint of the parish.

Inside, the church's chief treasure is the reredos of St Anne, mother of the Virgin Mary – a baroque riot of painted and gilded woodcarving, dating from 1682. In the central panel, the Virgin and St Anne sit contemplating a standing figure of the infant Christ, between columns decorated with climbing vines. Saints,

*At 380 metres above sea level, Montagne Saint-Michel, set in wild heathland, is almost the highest point in Brittany. It is crowned by a chapel to St Michael, the patron saint of high places.*

cherubs, garlands and swags of fruit add to the overall impression of lavish exuberance. The rector of the day, 'Missire Yves Mesager', has left his name prominently displayed on the reredos; but its carver is unknown. A guidebook to Commana makes the likely suggestion that he was a master-craftsman from the Brest ship-yards, skilled in carving figureheads and other decorative woodwork for Louis XIV's men-of-war.

From Commana you can continue due west to Sizun – another small town with a remarkable parish close – along the D764. But the three prize closes of the region, grouped and signposted as the Circuit des Trois Enclos, are 30 kilometres north of Commana, and are not to be missed. So first return to the D785, follow it north through Pleyber-Christ, then head west on the D712.

Saint-Thégonnec, the easternmost of the three, represents the final flowering of the *enclos* tradition, and is far grander in conception than the closes we have so far seen. The triumphal arch, which stands on massively solid piers, was built about 1590 and is the oldest element in the scheme. The ossuary is as large and ornate as many village churches; built a century later than the arch but still in renaissance style, its main façade has a double row of pilasters, which frame windows on the lower level and shell-shaped niches above. Inside the ossuary is a highly naturalistic Entombment made of carved and painted oak from about 1700, with life-sized figures of saints round the body of Christ.

The church is a majestic building, with a lofty renaissance-style tower sprouting a central cupola and small corner cupola-turrets. The main body was not completed until well into the eighteenth century; among its treasures are the pulpit, swirling with angels and allegorical figures, the intricate choir stalls, and the lavish baroque high altar.

*The interior of Guimiliau church. The organ and the font canopy, both lavishly decorated with carved woodwork, date from the 1670s.*

*A carved figure of a saint from the mangificently painted and gilded seventeenth-century reredos of St Anne in Commana church.*

Saint-Thégonnec's granite calvary is a fascinating combination of the moving and the grotesque. The figures of Christ, the two thieves and the mourning Marys stand on columns high above the low plinth; below them are carvings of scenes from the Passion – Christ being scourged, Pilate washing his hands – which are more like three-dimensional caricatures than attempts at realistic portrayal. One of Christ's tormentors is said to represent Henri IV, whose conversion to Catholicism in 1593 with the words 'Paris is worth a mass' was regarded as sheer hypocrisy by the fervently religious Bretons. Presumably Henry is the grinning moustached figure, dressed in knee-breeches and fringed jerkin, who is pulling on one end of a cord passed round Christ's wrists.

Thégonnec himself is an obscure fifth-century figure, described by a chronicler as a saint 'whose acts

The parish close at Saint-Thégonnec, a fine example of a type of architectural complex found only in Finistère. Such closes consist of a parish church, a triumphal entrance arch, a calvary carved with the Crucifixion story, and an ossuary or mortuary chapel for the bones of the dead.

*Details from Finistère's parish closes.* TOP LEFT *Christ in bonds, from the calvary at Saint-Thégonnec.* TOP RIGHT *The Ankou (the Breton figure of death) in La Martyre church.* BOTTOM LEFT *The Pietà on the calvary at Brasparts.* BOTTOM RIGHT *Christ washing the disciples' feet, Plougastel-Daoulas.*

we have no record of'. His statue on the calvary shows him with a wagon hauled by a stag and an ox, referring to the legend that he built the first church at Saint-Thégonnec with stone from the hills, quarrying it and bringing it down himself.

Guimiliau, the central close of the three, exhibits all the elements of an *enclos* more perfectly than any other in Brittany. The church, reached through a triumphal arch simple in design, is amazingly rich on the outside and even more ornate internally. Built in the early seventeenth century, it has an elaborate porch carved round the archway with scenes from the Bible and lined with brightly coloured statues of saints. Inside the church is a profusion of carved and painted reredoses, statues and other woodwork, and an organ by the English builder Thomas Dallam, active in Brittany in the mid seventeenth century. But the masterpiece at Guimiliau is its sixteenth-century calvary; built to an X-shaped ground plan, to give the sculptors more room for their creations, it supports a double row of over 200 carved figures taken both from the Bible and from Breton legend.

Though the calvary is now four centuries old, its hard granite has scarcely been affected by those hundreds of winters and thousands of rainstorms, apart from taking on the blotches and lichens of age. Incongruous among the figures of the disciples and the Holy Family is the carving of the Three Holy Women, who watch over the burial at the foot of the cross. The right-hand figure is dressed in detail as a sixteenth-century court lady, and is said to be a portrait of Mary Queen of Scots, who was executed in 1587, about the date of the calvary. If it is indeed a memorial to her, it would be hard to imagine a more graceful tribute. Elsewhere on the calvary one of Brittany's legendary temptresses is portrayed in a sinister tableau, no doubt designed to keep the girls of the parish on the straight and narrow: Katell Gollet ('Catherine the Damned'), renowned for her immorality, is being dragged and goaded down to hell, here represented as a gaping mouth of stone.

Guimiliau means 'the parish of St Miliau', and we meet this saint again at nearby Lampaul-Guimiliau, the third close on the circuit. (The other half of the name, Lampaul, means 'religious settlement of St Pol'.) Miliau was a sixth-century prince of Cornouaille, in southwest Finistère, heir to his father's throne, and famous for his benevolence. In the course of a quarrel over the succession, his brother cut off his head, whereupon Miliau picked it up from the ground, while his severed neck gushed with blood. On the strength of this grisly miracle, he was revered as a martyr and was canonized.

The most notable feature of the church at Lampaul-Guimiliau is its curious sawn-off spire, 70m high when it was first built in 1573 but truncated by lightning in 1809 and never rebuilt. The triumphal arch, ossuary and calvary are simple in comparison with those found elsewhere; but the church is well worth visiting for its profusion of magnificent carved woodwork. The sixteenth-century rood-beam, surmounted by a painted Crucifixion, is carved with a painted frieze showing the Passion in vivid strip-cartoon form; the arms of the choir stalls are carved with gaping sea monsters; and there are several elaborate altars and reredoses. The two saints from which the village gets its name are also portrayed. In the ossuary a painted statue of St Pol shows him leading a dragon he has tamed by a stole tied round its neck; and on an altar panel in the church St Miliau appears in princely robes holding his head, while his wicked brother, in boots, spurs and cocked hat, sheathes his sword as he prepares for his getaway on a white horse.

If you have not yet had your fill of parish closes, drive south for Sizun along the D11, turning right in the village of Saint-Sauveur. Sizun's towering spire, 60m high, is visible from miles away; it dates from about 1730, and is thus a good deal later than the rest of the complex. The unique triple-arched triumphal arch was built in the 1580s, as was the ossuary, gravely classical in feeling, with its row of bearded saints

*The sixteenth-century rood beam in the church of Lampaul-Guimiliau is brilliantly painted with scenes from the Passion story.*

filling the upper niches of the façade. The ossuary has been turned into a small museum, with a display of Breton furniture such as a box bed (*lit-clos*). Inside the church, the brightly painted and gilded statues, altars and reredoses make it one of the most exuberant of Breton church interiors. The organ is exceptionally fine, as is its gallery painted with *trompe-l'oeil* balustrading.

My favourite among all the parish closes comes at the end of this zigzag quest across Finistère. La Martyre, along a byroad off the D764, is one of the oldest of them all, dating mainly from the mid fifteenth century. It has a time-ravaged beauty that is far more moving than the spruced-up appearance of later and better-maintained examples. Its presiding genius is a Dutchman, Fons de Kort, who lives in an ancient house by the church, and has devoted half a lifetime to unravelling the architectural and historical mysteries of La Martyre.

Its name, which means 'The Martyrdom', is said to derive from the martyred Salomon or Salaün, a ninth-century king of Brittany, who in 857 won the throne by murdering his cousin Erispoë. After a reign of fifteen years he retired to a hermitage in the forest, where he was hunted down by partisans of Erispoë. Bursting into the church where he was praying, they stabbed his young son before his eyes, then blinded Salomon and cut off his head. Though his life had scarcely been saintly, he was canonized soon after his death, and revered subsequently throughout Brittany as one of the greatest of its rulers. La Martyre was a well-established shrine by the early Middle Ages, and its tower may date as far back as the eleventh century. By the fifteenth century it was the centre of a huge annual fair, which attracted merchants from all over Europe, and brought enough wealth to the little town to finance extensive building.

What strikes the eye at La Martyre is not so much the overall appearance of the church and its surroundings, which are close-knit and not easy to appreciate as a whole, as the detail, and in particular the porch and ossuary that stand side by side at the main entrance. The south porch of La Martyre is one of the marvels of Brittany. Carved with angels, peasants and coats of arms, it is crowned by a tender Nativity, which even in its present mutilated state is a touching and beautiful work of art. The Virgin was originally shown suckling her child with her breasts bare; but at some stage child and breasts were hacked away – perhaps by some puritanical clergyman – and the Virgin's arms now cradle a flat expanse of stone.

The scenes on either side of the porch are full of down-to-earth sketches of Breton life, like the hooded peasants playing *crosse* (a kind of primitive hockey or golf), while an angel announces the Nativity overhead. Here and there on the stonework Fons de Kort has found traces of paint, which shows that the whole porch must once have been coloured as brilliantly as a medieval manuscript. As always in Brittany, death was close at hand in the shape of the skeletal figure of the Ankou, who is carved above the holy-water stoup holding a severed head. Inside the church are some good grotesque capitals. The painted wall-plates below the ceiling are carved with charming vignettes of bagpipe players, a plough pulled by a joint team of horses and oxen, and scenes from the Nativity.

Next to the porch, and echoing its general shape in the renaissance style of the early seventeenth century, is the ossuary, originally painted gold and blue. Over the door are angels holding scrolls, inscribed in Breton with the grim message: 'Death, judgment, cold hell, when a man thinks upon it he must tremble. Foolish is he who does not meditate upon these things, knowing that he must die.' A curious feature is the Egyptian-looking caryatid at the corner.

Over the past fifteen years I have been to La Martyre on four occasions, and each time have been struck by the dilapidation of the church, though there is some limited restoration work currently going on. On my most recent visit the village street had been prettified

*The extraordinary Pont de Rohan across the River Elorn, in the centre of Landerneau. The houses on it date from the sixteenth century.*

by having its tarmac taken up and a neat stone and brick surface laid in its stead; the money would surely have been far better spent on the church than on unnecessary road embellishment. I was told in a bar in La Martyre that the resurfacing was carried out because the mayor of the village did not want to be outdone by the mayor of Locronan, who had just resurfaced his own little town – but that may have been just bar-room gossip.

From La Martyre, continue west to Landerneau, a spacious riverside town, at the point where the Elorn estuary narrows to a bridgeable width. For centuries it was an important port and commercial centre, and the capital of the region of Léon. Medieval trade links with England are recalled by the dedication of the church south of the river, which is to St Thomas of Canterbury (Thomas Becket). No doubt English cloth-merchants visiting the trade fairs at centres such as La Martyre made Landerneau their headquarters. Its ancient bridge, the Pont de Rohan, links two bishoprics, Léon to the north and Cornouaille to the south; unusually, the houses built on it in the sixteenth century have never been cleared away in the interests of modern traffic. A traditional expression, *Ça fera du bruit dans Landerneau* ('That will make a noise in Landerneau'), is said to derive from the local practice of making an uproar outside the house of any widow who decided to remarry.

Drive south from Landerneau to Daoulas along the D770, a fine road across rolling, open countryside. Daoulas is something of a forgotten treasure, bypassed by the Quimper-Brest motorway. A steep street of granite houses, the Rue de l'Eglise, leads up to a grand romanesque abbey church at the top of the hill; it is approached through a curious triumphal arch-cum-belfry, hung with two huge bells. Tucked away behind the church are the abbey ruins and gardens. A good deal survives of the twelfth-century cloister, where excavations are currently going on; when I went there an archaeologist had just unearthed a seventeenth-century skeleton from under the cloister floor. Elsewhere in the gardens are a beautiful fountain and a small oratory with an altar dated 1737. The trees are labelled with their names in Latin, French and Breton, as are the plants in the physic garden of medicinal herbs.

Like Landerneau, Daoulas was a centre of the medieval cloth trade, and the name daoulas or dowlas was given to a kind of coarse linen much in use in the sixteenth and seventeenth centuries. The term was well known to Shakespeare: in *Henry IV Part I* (III.iii), when Mistress Quickly tells Falstaff that he owes her money for shirts she has bought him, he answers: 'Dowlas, filthy dowlas: I have given them away to bakers' wives, and they have made bolters of them'. (A bolter was a sieve used for flour.) Shakespeare's father, who was a glover and presumably involved in the cloth trade, may well have visited the fair at La Martyre to buy his raw materials.

From Daoulas, head west for Brest along the N165, turning off after 15 kilometres for Plougastel-Daoulas. Outside the church in the centre of the little town is one of the finest calvaries in Brittany, built about 1600 after an outbreak of plague. It has more figures than any other calvary except the one at Guimiliau, which probably inspired it. As at Guimiliau, Katell Gollet appears, being dragged down to hell; among the saints portrayed are Saints Roch and Sebastian, who ward off epidemics, placed on the calvary as a safeguard against plague in the future. The peninsula on which Plougastel-Daoulas stands has an exceptionally mild climate and is Brittany's chief centre for strawberries, introduced here from Virginia towards the end of the eighteenth century.

The N165 to Brest crosses the Elorn over a splendid bridge, which gives magnificent and contrasting views, upstream along the green estuary valley, and downstream to the cranes and skyscrapers of North France's major naval port. But the eye is first taken by

*The calvary at Plougastel-Daoulas, one of the finest in Brittany, was carved about 1600 as a thank-offering at the end of an outbreak of plague. It includes about 150 figures.*

the close-packed masts of the marina (Port de Plaisance) in the foreground, and behind them by the white, flattened pyramid of a futuristic-looking modern building.

Before braving the traffic of Brest's city centre, turn off the main road for Océanopolis, as the building is called. Standing on reclaimed ground behind the marina, its aim is to explain the world of the sea to the people of Brest and the surrounding area, who are no doubt more in need of such explanation than their maritime ancestors. Beneath its wide expanses of glass you can steer a miniature fleet by remote control, listen to the recorded squeaks and rumbles of dolphins and whales, study exhibitions showing the marine life of the Breton coast – or just enjoy the sight of dozens of Brest families having a good time in a high-tech, imaginative environment.

Océanopolis dates from 1990; but the history of Brest goes back at least 2000 years earlier. The Rade ('roadstead') de Brest is one of Europe's most superb natural harbours, stretching from the Elorn Estuary to the easily defended narrows, less than 2 kilometres wide, of the Goulet de Brest, and protected from the Atlantic swell by the triple-pronged Crozon peninsula. Brest grew up along the banks of the narrow Penfeld river, guarded by the spur on which its château is built. It was certainly a maritime centre in pre-Roman times. The Romans fortified it; during the Middle Ages it was much fought over; and it began to take on its modern importance under Louis XIV in the seventeenth century, when it became the chief port of the French navy. It reached the height of its prosperity with the advent of the railway and steam-powered ships in the nineteenth century, expanding east and west along the Rade de Brest from the banks of the Penfeld.

During World War II Brest was largely obliterated, first by Allied bombing, but mainly at the time of the Liberation in 1944, when the Germans put up a last-ditch defence, and were only defeated after a siege of six weeks, followed by savage house-to-house fighting. So it is now virtually a post-war town, consisting mainly of wide streets of white concrete buildings. Nevertheless, it is worth more than a passing glance, as it is as typical of the new forward-looking Brittany as towns like Morlaix are of the historic past.

What is left of old Brest is best seen from the mighty Pont de Récouvrance across the Penfeld, the largest vertical-lift bridge in Europe, with its two H-shaped pylons from which the central span is suspended. Upstream is the Arsénal Maritime, the naval dockyard, which stretches along both sides of the river and can only be visited by French citizens. Looking downstream, on the right is the medieval Tour Tanguy, now a small museum, and on the left the castle, which as Brest's only surviving major historic monument is the most interesting place to begin an exploration of the town.

The château is a large complex of buildings, with broad landscaped terraces separating the various layers of fortification, which rise sheer from the water. Much of it is occupied by the Préfecture Maritime, but a number of the massive medieval towers – Tour Madeleine, Tour de Paradis, Tour Duchesse Anne – are given over to the collections of the Musée Maritime. There are any number of ship models, figureheads, drawings and plans of Brest in the time of Louis XIV, and portraits of long-forgotten admirals; while the terraces between one tower and the next give wide and varying panoramas across the Rade de Brest. An unexpectedly modern touch is the 10m wooden cockleshell in which no fewer than forty 'boat people' escaped from Vietnam in 1988.

A good circular walk from the château takes you along the Cours Dajot, a tree-shaded esplanade above the Port de Commerce. At one end is a small garden celebrating French victories over the English in the American War of Independence in 1780–81, and at the other a tall pink granite obelisk honouring the *hauts faits* ('high deeds') of the navies of the United States and France in World War I. There is no mention of the

*Cranes and quayside buildings line the commercial harbour of Brest, which has been a maritime centre since pre-Roman times.*

British navy's contribution – but no doubt the esplanade should be regarded as pro-American rather than anti-British. The road that runs alongside is called the Rue Denver, after Denver, Colorado, which is twinned with Brest.

From the esplanade, walk inland via the wide Square Président John Kennedy to the Place de la Liberté, at the top of the town. From here the Rue de Siam, the spinal column of Brest, leads downhill in a dead straight line back to the Récouvrance bridge and the château. Formerly called the Rue Saint-Pierre, it got its present exotic-sounding name in 1686, when ambassadors from the Siamese court landed at Brest on their way to meet Louis XIV. The Rue de Siam is partly pedestrianized, and is the gathering-place of such eccentrics as Brest can muster. When I last walked down it, an English girl was lecturing Brest on its need to return to God, each sentence being translated into French by her stentorian-voiced male companion; but Brest was taking little notice.

The visit of the Siamese ambassadors features, along with other major events in the town's history, in a diorama in the conical-roofed Tour Tanguy, across the bridge from the château. Built in the fifteenth century by Tanguy de Chastel, one of the most powerful Bretons of his time, it is now a museum, with exhibits that include models of old Brest, a fine collection of early photographs, and notable nineteenth-century engravings of scenes from convict life. For more than a century from 1750 much of the left bank of the Penfeld was occupied by an enormous *bagne* or prison, which housed over 2000 convicts and provided the labour to build the dockyards and other harbour works. Gustave Flaubert saw it around 1850, and has left a sombre description:

These heaps of cannons, cannonballs and anchors, these huge straight workshops full of screeching machinery, the continuous clank of the chains of the convicts, passing row on row and working in silence – all this sinister, pitiless, unnatural mechanism, this heaping-up of organised mistrust, soon weighs down your spirits with its tedium and wearies the sight.

If any *bagnard* succeeded in escaping, the countryside round about would be alerted by gunfire, nicknamed *tonnerre de Brest* ('Brest thunder'). Fleeing through hostile country, and easily identifiable from his yellow trousers and the letters TF (*travaux forcés*, 'forced labour') branded on his shoulder, he was almost certain to be picked up within a few hours. Instead of tracker dogs, the prison authorities used the local gypsies, who knew every inch of the countryside, and relied for their income on their success in recapturing prisoners. For the convict, recapture meant a return to floggings, leg irons and the chain gang. In 1864 the *bagne* was closed and its inmates transferred to Devil's Island, off the coast of South America, where – unlike at Brest – the brutalities they endured were out of sight and out of mind.

From Brest, take the D789 through seemingly endless suburbs to the westernmost point of the Breton mainland. The Pointe de Saint-Mathieu is a suitably commanding headland for its strategic position at the entrance to the Rade de Brest, and not surprisingly it is the site of a lighthouse. What is surprising is to see the lighthouse looming above the ruins of a medieval abbey; from certain angles it looks as though it is piercing through the roof. The abbey of Saint-Mathieu is said to have been founded in the sixth century; it gets its name from the legend that Breton sailors brought the body of St Matthew from Egypt, and built a church to receive it. At some stage the body was stolen, but the skull was returned in 1206, and the abbey became a place of pilgrimage. The monks earned their keep by maintaining a light on the abbey tower, forerunner of the present lighthouse. After the Revolution the abbey was abandoned and its buildings were used as a quarry, but enough survives – notably the soaring arches of the nave – to give an idea of Saint-

*Brest's Pont de Récouvrance, across the River Penfeld, is the largest vertical-lift bridge in Europe. On the left is the conical roof of the medieval Tour Tanguy, one of the city's few ancient buildings.*

Mathieu's past glories, when monks chanted the office on their lonely headland, and the great west window reflected the light of the setting sun to the glittering sea below.

The parapet of the lighthouse provides a staggering view, westward across the reefs to the distant islands of Molène and Ouessant (Ushant), south-east to the broken coast of the Crozon peninsula, and due south to the Pointe du Raz. Directly below is a seagull's-eye view of the shattered roof of the abbey church. A small museum on the site has some carved stone fragments from the abbey, and documents relating to its history. On the seaward side of the abbey is a tall granite monument to sailors from Brittany who died at sea in World War I, carved with a mourning mother in a Breton *coiffe*.

Le Conquet, 4 kilometres north of Saint-Mathieu and mainland Brittany's most westerly town, is the jumping-off point for Ouessant. It is a pretty little port built on the southern side of a quiet estuary, with a small fishing fleet that lives from its catches of lobsters and crayfish. Though it is ancient in origin (its old Breton name is Konk-Léon, the 'Creek of Léon'), not much of the historic town survives, as it was largely burnt down by the English in 1558.

In spite of modern transport, Ouessant is still one of the remotest and least-spoilt corners of Brittany, and is protected from the ravages of unchecked development by being an offshoot of the Parc Naturel Régional d'Armorique. Throughout the year a pair of sturdy little passenger ferries make the hour-long crossing to the island from Le Conquet, across 20 kilometres of Europe's most treacherous waters. Several lighthouses and dozens of black-and-yellow buoys mark the reefs that at low tide break the surface like rotten teeth, and at high tide lurk under the water, ready to tear the bottom out of any boat that tries to sail over them. On a fine summer's day, with the sun glinting on the water and the surf lapping gently against the rocks, the crossing seems easy enough. But when gales hurl the waves high over the lighthouses, or fog comes rolling in from the Atlantic, it is easy to understand how the sea round Ouessant was a place of dread during the centuries of sail, and remains so even in these days of sophisticated radar navigation.

The island was well known to the earliest geographers and navigators. Pytheas, the Greek navigator who about 330 BC sailed round much of western Europe, called it Ouxisame; Pliny the Elder, writing in the first century AD, knew it as Axantos; to Ptolemy a century later it was Uxantisima. Its Breton name, Enez Eussa (Eussa Island), is derived from the Celtic deity Eus, the god of terror; though a more prosaic etymology derives it from an an ancient Celtic word meaning either 'the farthest' or 'the highest'. Both are applicable to Ouessant, as it is the westernmost point not just of Brittany but of France as well, and much the highest island of its small archipelago.

Throughout the crossing from Le Conquet the Ouessant coast is visible. It is crowned at its highest point by a giant minaret-like radar tower, built in the 1980s in the wake of oil-tanker disasters off the Finistère coast. The boat lands you at Port Stiff, a small creek below the radar tower, where dozens of bicycles are lined up for hire. Cycling is easily the best way to explore the island, as though it is only about 7 kilometres long by 4 wide, the roads – mostly little more than tracks – are never the shortest distance between two points. There is no chance of getting lost, as Ouessant has hardly any trees, and there is always a lighthouse in view (sometimes two or three at once) to show you where you are.

One of them, the Phare du Créac'h, is the island's main tourist attraction. The building at its foot is now a display centre devoted to explaining the workings of lighthouses, buoys and the coast in general (Centre d'Interprétation des Phares et Balises). All round the hall the facets of rotating lighthouse lenses flash with hundreds of twinkling diamond points, like strobe lighting on some huge and silent dance floor. Displays

*The lighthouse and ruined abbey on the end of the Pointe de Saint-Mathieu, at the western extremity of northern Finistère.*

round the walls show the evolution of lighthouse construction from Roman times, along with such historical details as the seventeenth-century penalty for wreckers who lured ships to their doom: they were executed, and hung on a ship's mast at the scene of their crime.

The rocks below Créac'h are an ideal spot from which to watch the birds that make Ouessant an ornithologist's paradise. Puffins, storm petrels and gannets breed round its fragmented shores, and almost 350 species have been recorded during the spring and autumn migrations.

A few hundred metres away across the interior-sprung turf, grazed smooth by the native black sheep, is Ouessant's little Ecomusée, in two low, stone-built cottages. One contains a small museum of costumes and local life, while the other is furnished as the house of a sailor's family around the turn of the century. Box-beds, cupboards, tables, statues of the Virgin, photographs and cooking utensils are all neatly stowed in a tiny two-roomed space more reminiscent of a couple of cabins on board ship than a family house. The furniture is all made of driftwood, and is painted in the Virgin's colours of blue and white.

More often than not, only women and children, and men past seafaring age, would be at home, as the able-bodied men spent most of their time away at sea. So the island developed into something of a matriarchy, where it was the custom for the women to run everyday affairs, and even to propose marriage, when it would have been unthinkable on the mainland. Until the nineteenth century a unique courting ritual took place. When a Ouessant girl decided to get married, she would take a piece of bacon to the house of the young man of her choice. Forewarned of her arrival, he stayed in bed, and she offered him the bacon. If he accepted, the girl would move into the boy's house for a

probationary period, helping her future mother-in-law in the fields and about the house. Not until this period was over was the marriage held and consummated.

Another unique custom was the *proella* – a funeral rite held for Ouessant sailors who had died far from home. When news of such a death reached the island, the mayor told the dead man's godfather, who passed it on to the neighbourhood. Last of all, at nightfall, he called at the house of the dead man's widow or mother, giving her the ritual message: 'A *proella* will be held here this evening, my poor child.' She then laid out a linen cross with a small wax cross on top, and a vigil and prayers were held round it all night long. The next day the wax cross (*croix de proella*) was taken to the church at Lampaul, Ouessant's main village, placed for a time in an urn beside the altar, and finally added to the crosses in a small hut-shaped mausoleum in the crowded cemetery below the church. The mausoleum is still there, with an inscription to 'our sailors who died far from home, by war, disease or shipwreck'.

Ouessant's history has been punctuated by tragedies off its own rocky coast. One of the worst disasters took place in the summer of 1896, on a June night of dead calm, when Ouessant and the neighbouring island of Molène were enveloped in fog. A British passenger ship, the *Drummond Castle*, struck a reef west of Molène, and ten minutes later went bow-first to the bottom; there were only three survivors. In gratitude for the islanders' heroic though futile efforts to save passengers and crew, Queen Victoria gave a chalice to Molène's church, and paid for a new spire for the church in Lampaul.

Back on the mainland, the coast road (D28) runs north of Le Conquet for 20 kilometres through open countryside, broken only at the village of Plouarzel. In 1988 Plouarzel qualified for the *Guinness Book of Records* by cooking the world's biggest pancake, 6 metres across and weighing two tonnes. A few kilometres inland is the Menhir de Kerloas, at 12m high the tallest monolith in France. In spite of its size, it is easy to miss, as it is some way from the road and reached along a field path. About a metre from the ground are boss-shaped protuberances, against which young

---

*Lobster-pots neatly lined up beside the harbour at Le Conquet, the starting point for the ferry trip to the wind-swept island of Ouessant (Ushant).*

wives anxious to conceive a child used to rub themselves – the kind of pagan fertility custom which was stamped out elsewhere in Europe by Christianity, but lingered on in remote areas.

When I went to Plouarzel, I took the wrong road out of the village, and was glad to have done so, as my mistake took me past the dainty sixteenth-century chapel of Saint-Eloi (Eligius), which lies at the end of an avenue of trees, miles from anywhere beside the Ildut river. Inside the chapel is a small wooden statue of Eligius, the patron saint of blacksmiths, holding hammer and pincers, with a miniature horse beside him. Like several other Breton saints, in the seventh century he is said to have sailed across the Channel from Britain in a stone trough. On June 24 a *pardon* for horses and their owners is held at Saint-Eloi; a ditch has been dug from the nearby pilgrims' fountain, so that the animals have somewhere to drink.

The coast road crosses the muddy Ildut estuary and continues round to the small town of Ploudalmézeau. Three kilometres before you get there, a side road leads down to the harbour of Portsall, facing north across a sea studded with islets and reefs. It was off this coast, in March 1978, that the supertanker *Amoco Cadiz* ran aground and broke up, disgorging a quarter of a million tons of oil into the sea. All along the northern coast, from the Rade de Brest to the Bay of St Brieuc, the *marée noire* ('black tide') soaked into the sand of the holiday beaches, blackened the rocks, filled every little pool and crevice, and left an oily froth marking the limit of each succeeding wave. Three weeks after the catastrophe I explored the area, and found a coast that stank like a petrol station and was almost totally without seabirds, apart from a few sick-looking gulls with oil-fouled wings and bellies. Out at sea, what was left of the tanker's hull could just be made out through the offshore mist.

Returning to Portsall after a lapse of a dozen years, I could hardly believe that the disaster had ever happened. The wreck had vanished, the rocks were clean and covered in fresh weed, the gulls were back in force, and children were digging for bait in the estuary mud. Yet Portsall has not forgotten the *Amoco Cadiz*:

28 tons of anchor and rusty chain have been hauled up from the seabed and placed on the harbour wall, like some monstrous piece of modern sculpture.

To complete the round of the Côte des Abers (*aber* means 'estuary' in Breton, as it does in Welsh), follow the D28 across the Aber Benoît and Aber Wrac'h estuaries, where at low tide hulks and small boats lie stranded on the mud. At Plouguerneau, a small Musée Maritime recalls the past of the Abers, with exhibits on the shaping of the coast, on lighthouses, and on the back breaking toil of the *goémoniers* (seaweed-gatherers), which is still carried on today. The Phare de l'Ile Vierge, 5 kilometres north-west of the village, is the world's tallest stone-built lighthouse

From Plouguerneau, head inland along the D32 to Le Folgoët. The spire of its huge basilica comes into view across the maize fields when you are still 5 kilometres or more away, and its cathedral-like scale in a country-side of small village chapels shows that you are reaching a major religious centre. Le Folgoët (Ar Folgoat in Breton) means 'the Fool in the Wood', and arises from a typically Breton meeting of fact and fantasy.

In the mid fourteenth century a simpleton called Salomon or Salaün lived beside a spring in a wood, outside the neighbouring town of Lesneven. Every morning he would come into Lesneven, where he attended mass, continually intoning the words *O Itroun Gwerhez Mari* ('O Lady Virgin Mary'), and was given food by the inhabitants. Back in the wood, he would dip his bread in the spring to soften it; and in the depths of winter he would jump in the water up to his armpits, then climb a tree and shake the branches, shouting *O Mari!* as he did so. Not surprisingly, the locals called him Salaün-ar-Foll, Salomon the Mad. He died in about 1358. Soon after, a white lily grew from his grave, with the words AVE MARIA inscribed in gold

---

*The anchor and chain of the oil tanker* Amoco Cadiz, *beside the harbour at Portsall. The ship ran aground off north-west Finistère in 1978 and broke up, polluting much of the north Brittany coast.*

on its petals. Curious to discover where the miraculous flower came from, the clergy dug down to its roots, and found that it was growing from the mouth of Salaün.

Then politics took over, as often happened in medieval Brittany. Duke Jean IV of Brittany saw in the story of Salaün the means of securing the loyalty of the volatile Bretons of Finistère. He ordained that a chapel should be built on the spot, and laid the first stone himself in January 1365. The shrine of Le Folgoët was favoured by successive dukes and grew rich as a result, culminating in a visit by Duchess Anne during her tour of the whole of Brittany in 1506, when she financed the completion of the basilica.

The church, built in Flamboyant gothic style, has twin west towers of different sizes. The big north tower is crowned with a lofty spire and surrounding spirelets, but the southern one was never properly completed, and has a simple conical roof added in the seventeenth century. At the back of the church, below the east window, is the spring in which Salaün dipped his bread, and himself. The most notable feature of the interior is the magnificent and intricate stone rood-screen, extremely rare in Brittany, where wooden screens are the norm; its leaves and other motifs are carved with a lace-like delicacy. The story of Salaün is told in the windows at the eastern end; and later miracles are commemorated in other ways, such as the carved relief showing a rail crash in 1882, from which Bretons on their way to Lourdes escaped unharmed. The presbytery near the church contains a small local museum of Breton furniture, costumes and religious processional banners. Le Folgoët holds one of Brittany's most important *pardons*, on the first Sunday after September 8.

From Le Folgoët, drive through Lesneven and head east along the D788. Past the village of Lanhouarneau, fork right along back roads to Kerjean, the finest château in this part of Brittany. Unlike so many Breton castles, which seem to be gradually sinking into the

---

*The muddy estuary of Aber Wrac'h, one of a series of creeks that split the coast of north-west Finistère.*

ground in somnolent though romantic decay, Kerjean is well maintained, and is being systematically restored. Approached down a noble avenue of beech trees, its granite outer walls, pierced for cannon, rise from a dry moat. The austere outer fortifications are in contrast to the palatial renaissance building within. Many of its mullioned windows now lack glass and gaze down at the courtyard like sightless eyes, as one wing was burnt down in 1710 and never rebuilt.

Kerjean was built by the Barbier family, who in about 1500 bought land and an old manor-house in Léon. By the mid sixteenth century they had made enough money to set about constructing a splendid mansion, though an envious local landowner compared them to 'the giants who built the Tower of Babel'. By 1580 or so the château was complete, with spacious apartments built round three sides of a courtyard, and a wide walkway along the southern or entrance side. For two prosperous centuries the owners of Kerjean were the region's uncrowned rulers; but the Revolutionaries guillotined its heiress and turned it into a barracks for the National Guard, describing it as 'an ancient haunt of tyranny and feudalism'. Fortunately it was saved from destruction and survived the nineteenth century in a battered but viable condition. The State took it over in 1911, and since 1986 it has been one of Finistère's chief cultural centres.

Most of the main rooms are now open, and have been restored to some degree. The barrel-vaulted chapel has some fine wall-plates, carved about 1580; the kitchen, with its two huge chimneys, is full of copper utensils and pewter bowls; and the guardroom has a collection of stone statues from ancient calvaries. The cobbled stables are now used for exhibitions, which change from year to year.

A recent exhibition gave a fascinating insight into one of the byways of Breton culture – the religious missions, which began in the seventeenth century, and went on, astonishingly, into the 1940s. The travelling mission priests would go from parish to parish, preaching hell-fire and damnation below banners on which all the sins, and to a lesser extent the virtues, were graphically portrayed. The nineteenth-century banners showed sinners as peasants in Breton costume, with the sins in various animal guises clutching at their souls. By the 1920s the peasants had changed to businessmen and flappers; while on the latest banners, dating from 1945, such sins as going to the cinema and voting in elections (presumably for anti-clerical candidates) had been added to gluttony, lust and the rest.

From Kerjean, drive north on the D30 for Plouescat and the coast. You are now in the Ceinture Dorée – the 'golden belt' of rich agricultural land that runs along the coast as far as Saint-Pol-de-Léon, and grows the artichokes, cauliflowers and other vegetables that make this region one of the wealthiest in Brittany. At Plouescat, turn east along the D10 for Saint-Pol; just before the village of Sibiril, a lane to the left leads down to the Château de Kerouzéré. Unlike Kerjean, it is not in the public domain, and can only be seen by prior arrangement. Built in 1425 by Jean de Kerouzéré, it is a formidable-looking building, turreted and compact, with the rugged strength typical of a once-lawless region. Below the château is a flat expanse that looks like a tiltyard, and to the north is a glimpse of the sea in the distance.

As you approach Saint-Pol, you can see its spires rising above the artichoke fields. But make first for Roscoff, along the bypass, as Saint-Pol lies on the return road to Morlaix. Since the 1970s, the port installations south of Roscoff have become familiar to the thousands of British tourists crossing the Channel from Plymouth, most of whom are in a hurry to press on southwards and so miss out Roscoff altogether. This is their loss, as it is a pretty little town, with plenty to explore in its streets of granite houses. It has a long seafaring history, which reached its height in the days of the corsairs from the sixteenth to the eighteenth centuries. Many of the houses in the main square and along the seafront date from those great days. Above them rises Roscoff's extraordinary sixteenth-century church tower, with its perforated stonework, carefully graded stages and corner turrets. The two stone cannon that jut menacingly from its walls were reputedly to warn off potential English attackers.

The last time I went to Roscoff, I heard a lone musician playing his *bombarde* (Breton oboe) below the church walls. When he had finished the cheerful little tune, which he told me was called the Gavotte de Roscoff, he wandered off down the street, tootling away to anyone who cared to listen. By an odd coincidence, when I was in Lorient the following month, I heard a familiar solitary piping. It was my friend from Roscoff – a true wandering minstrel if ever I saw one – playing to the summer holiday crowds.

By the seafront, the remains of Roscoff's medieval town wall – now separated from the sea by a wide expanse of tarmac – carries a stone inscription stating that Mary Stuart (Mary Queen of Scots) landed at Roscoff in 1548. Aged only five, she was on her way from Scotland to Paris to be engaged to the Dauphin François, who was two years younger. She stayed in France for thirteen years, the happiest period of her tragic life. In April 1558 the young couple were married. The following September François succeeded to the throne as François II, but he died three months later at the age of sixteen. The widowed Mary returned to Scotland in 1561, to the glories and miseries of her later career.

On a house in Roscoff's square is a plaque carved with the beaky, bearded profile of Tristan Corbière, Roscoff's adopted poet. Born in Morlaix in 1845, Corbière was a consumptive, who alternated between two wildly different life-styles – in Paris, where he lived in a garret like a true Bohemian, and in Roscoff, where he retreated to the sea air for the good of his health. He died in 1875 aged only 29, leaving behind him a single book of poems, *Les Amours Jaunes*, much admired by later poets such as Verlaine. While at Roscoff he became a sailing fanatic, careering in his yacht up and down the narrow channel between

*The old town of Roscoff is dominated by the graded tiers of its unusual church tower. Roscoff has a long sea-faring history, and now rivals Saint-Malo as a cross-Channel port.*

Roscoff and the offshore Ile de Batz. His poems veer between celebrations of the night life of Paris and hymns to the sea. To Corbière, Roscoff was *une vieille coque bien ancrée* ('an old ship at anchor') and *une vieille fille des matelots* ('an old sailors' tart'), which cannot have pleased the town's more staid inhabitants.

As befits a place that has always looked towards the sea for its livelihood, Roscoff has one of France's most famous centres of marine biology. It was founded in 1872 by a Sorbonne zoology professor, Henri Lacaze-Duthiers, after whom Roscoff's main square is named. The Station Biologique is both an international graduate teaching centre, and an institute devoted to studying every aspect of the sea, from oceanography to the effects of pollution. At Roscoff's Thalassotherapy clinic – the first in France, founded in 1899 – visitors can combine the pleasures of a seaside holiday with the rigours of seaweed baths, high-pressure water jets and other marine aids to healthier living.

On Roscoff's southern outskirts, not far from the ferryport, are two contrasting attractions: what are claimed to be the world's largest fish-tanks (*viviers*); and a botanic garden in the form of a huge natural rockery, where prickly pears, fuchsias, acanthus and geraniums flourish in the hollows between a cluster of giant boulders.

Offshore is one of the most idyllic corners in this part of Brittany, an ideal place to spend a lazy summer afternoon. The Ile de Batz (pronounced 'Ba'), hardly more than ten minutes by ferry across a narrow sound from Roscoff's long jetty, is an island of miniature stone-walled fields manured with seaweed, of narrow paths leading down to saltings facing the mainland, of yuccas, cacti and other subtropical plants. Its nineteenth-century church has a reliquary containing some of the bones of St Pol, who died on the island in 596, at the immense age of 104. He is usually portrayed leading a dragon by his stole tied round its neck; the dragon was terrifying the neighbourhood, but St Pol succeeded in taming it, leading it to the end of Batz, and hitting it with his pastoral staff until it jumped into the sea and was seen no more.

The cathedral of Saint-Pol-de-Léon, 5 kilometres south of Roscoff, has more of the saint's relics – to be precise, his skull, finger and armbone, and his copper bell, which is said to prevent headaches if rung in the correct manner. The twin spires of this noble gothic building, dating mainly from the thirteenth and fourteenth centuries, tower above the main square of the town. Inside, apart from St Pol's relics, there are some sixteenth-century choir stalls, a succession of tombs of the Bishops of Léon – a line which came to an end at the Revolution – and a macabre collection of caskets containing the skulls (*chefs*) of Saint-Pol-de-Léon's notabilities down the years.

The cathedral's spires are dwarfed by the gigantic tower and spire of the fifteenth-century chapel known as the Kreisker, a few hundred metres down the road. Looking from a distance like a huge grandfather clock, it is 77m to its apex, and dominates the artichoke and cauliflower fields for miles around. I do not find it in the least beautiful, but it makes an extraordinary gothic exclamation-mark in a countryside with few vertical features.

From the centre of Saint-Pol, turn left under the walls of the Kreisker in the direction of Morlaix, leaving the main road (D58) for Carantec, a resort with several good beaches across the muddy Penzé estuary from Roscoff and Saint-Pol. The renaissance triumphal arch in front of the church is unusual in being asymmetrical, with two arches of different sizes. From Carantec, a pretty estuary road (D73), with bracken and trees on one side and the placid river on the other, takes you back to Morlaix.

*An ornately carved window-surround in the Place Lacaze-Duthiers, the main square of Roscoff. The square is named after the nineteenth-century professor who founded Roscoff's marine biology centre.*

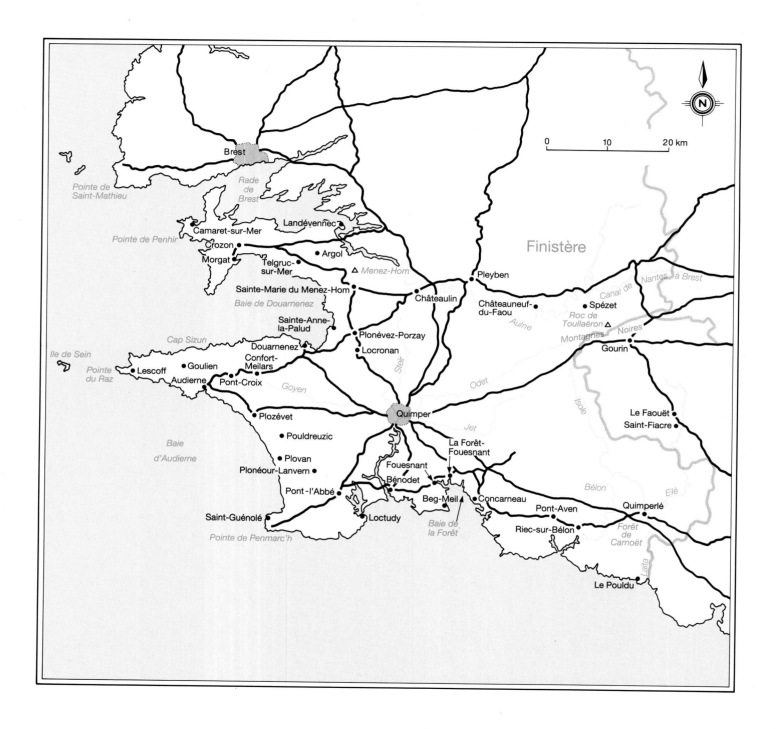

Brest

Pointe de
Saint-Mathieu

Rade
de
Brest

Pointe de Penhir

Camaret-sur-Mer

Landévennec

Crozon

Morgat

Telgruc-
sur-Mer

Argol

△ Menez-Hom

Finistère

Pleyben

Châteauneuf-
du-Faou

Spézet

Canal de

Nantes à Brest

Sainte-Marie du Menez-Hom

Châteaulin

Aulne

Baie de Douarnenez

Sainte-Anne-
la-Palud

Plonévez-Porzay

Locronan

Roc de
Toullaëron △

Montagnes

Noires

Gourin

Cap Sizun

Douarnenez

Confort-
Meilars

Steir

Odet

Ile de Sein

Pointe
du Raz

Lescoff

Goulien

Audierne

Pont-Croix

Goyen

Le Faouët

Saint-Fiacre

Plozévet

Quimper

Jet

Isole

Baie
d'Audierne

Pouldreuzic

Plovan

Plonéour-Lanvern

La Forêt-
Fouesnant

Bélon

Ellé

Pont-l'Abbé

Fouesnant

Bénodet

Beg-Meil

Concarneau

Pont-Aven

Quimperlé

Saint-Guénolé

Loctudy

Baie de
la Forêt

Riec-sur-Bélon

Forêt
de
Carnoët

Pointe de Penmarc'h

Laïta

Le Pouldu

0    10    20 km

N

# 4
# Cornouaille

*Quimper – Concarneau – Quimperlé – Gourin – Châteaulin*
*Camaret-sur-Mer – Douarnenez – Pointe du Raz*

Quimper is a delightful town, large enough to offer all the resources of an important provincial centre, yet not too large to be easily explored on foot. It is the capital both of Finistère and of that imprecise region of south-west Brittany known as Cornouaille, a name derived from Cornwall in England; its Breton name, Kemper, means 'river junction', and Quimper owed its early prosperity to its position at the junction of the Odet, which flows fast through the city centre, the Jet, and a third little stream, the Steïr, now channelled through a pipe along this part of its course.

The Odet divides Quimper's town centre neatly in two. On the north bank are the medieval cobbled streets, the noble twin-spired cathedral, and many of the public buildings; on the south, the steep slope of Mont Frugy, with alleys below it leading downstream to the ancient suburb of Locmaria, home of the famous Quimper Pottery. Until 1987 Frugy was covered in beech trees, which brought the illusion of an endless forest right into the heart of the town. But in October that year the great storm which also decimated the trees in the south of England passed over Brittany, doing untold damage, especially in Finistère. Fortunately the Quimpérois did not sit back in face of the

disaster: when I went back to the town less than three years after the storm, Frugy had been planted with saplings, and by the end of this century will no doubt be as good as new.

The area has been inhabited since prehistoric times, and the Romans had a colony at Locmaria. Quimper itself traces its origins back to a period a little later than the Romans: to the earliest days of Brittany, in the fourth and fifth centuries, and to the two semi-mythical figures of St Corentin and King Gradlon.

Corentin was born about 375, and spent much of his early life as a hermit in the forest below Menez-Hom, the mountain that guards the Crozon peninsula. Here he was kept alive by a miraculous fish, which obligingly let him cut a piece off it each day, and regenerated itself overnight. The miracle was witnessed by King Gradlon, who was out hunting and asked the saint for something to eat. Corentin cut a small piece off the back of his fish, which was enough for the king and his whole court. Naturally impressed, Gradlon first of all endowed Corentin with a monastery, and then offered him the bishopric of his new town of Kemper-Odetz, later called Kemper-Corentin. The cathedral is dedicated to him.

Gradlon too must have had some basis in fact. Like King Arthur, he may have been a post-Roman warlord who fought off the Norse invaders and then ruled over Quimper. But he is best known as the unhappy ruler of the sunken city of Ys, whose church bells can still be heard ringing below the waters of the Bay of Douarnenez. (It was this story which inspired Debussy's well known piano prelude *La Cathédrale Engloutie*, composed in 1910.)

The legend tells how Gradlon was betrayed through the wiles of his daughter Dahut or Ahès. The city of Ys was protected from the waves by sluice gates which could only be opened by a key that the king kept round his neck. But Dahut fell in love with the Devil, who persuaded her to take the key from her father's neck while he was asleep. The sluice gates were opened, the sea flooded in, and the city of Ys was drowned – all except King Gradlon, who escaped on his horse Morvarc'h (meaning 'horse of the sea' in Breton). In desperation Dahut clung to the horse behind her father, but as the waves threatened to overwhelm them, Gradlon thrust her into the waters and came safe to land.

Gradlon, mounted on Morvarc'h, still surveys his city from the parapet between the towers of the cathedral. The original statue is said to have been put there in the fifteenth century, but it was smashed in the Revolution, and the present one is a copy. Until the Revolution the Quimpérois kept up an ancient custom which no doubt originated in some prehistoric cult of dead kings. On the eve of St Cecilia's Day (November 22) the cathedral choir would stand on the balcony beside the statue and sing an anthem, while a town official (the *valet de ville*) climbed on to the horse behind the stone king, holding a bottle, a glass and a napkin. He tied the napkin round Gradlon's neck, filled the glass and held it to the king's lips. Then he drank the wine himself and hurled the glass into the square below, where the crowd fought to catch it before it smashed on the ground. No one ever won the prize of 100 *écus* offered to the successful catcher. The ceremony ended with a laurel branch placed like a sceptre in Gradlon's hand.

The cathedral's graceful twin spires dominate Quimper from every direction. Although they look as though they must have been there for centuries, they were built as recently as 1854. Before that, the towers were capped by low pyramidal roofs covered in slates, known disparagingly as 'St Corentin's candle-snuffers' (*éteignoirs*). The cathedral is one of the finest and most elaborate gothic buildings in Brittany, dating mainly from the thirteenth century. An unusual feature is the pronounced irregularity of the angle between the axes of the thirteenth-century nave and the fifteenth-century choir, often said to symbolize the drooping angle of Christ's head on the cross, but more probably because the choir is built on the site of an eleventh-century chapel, while the nave is on the different alignment of an earlier romanesque church.

The interior is sombre, darkened by heavily coloured stained glass, some of it dating from the fifteenth century. The finest of the furnishings is the organ, which rises above a stone screen; it was reconstructed in 1643 by Robert Dallam, a leading English organ-builder who had emigrated to Brittany the previous year, perhaps because of the Puritans' hostile attitude to music. He returned to England in 1660, at the Restoration, leaving his sons Thomas and Toussaint to carry on his work. Apart from Quimper, the Dallams were responsible for rebuilding the organs at Guimiliau, Sizun and Pleyben. The cathedral is currently undergoing a major restoration programme, and the east end, including the choir, is under wraps; the work is not expected to be finished until 1993–94.

Quimper is a town for strolling around as the spirit takes you, and does not lend itself to any kind of planned circular walk. Between the cathedral close and the river runs a stretch of the old town wall, strongly fortified, where the bishops of Quimper used to walk and enjoy the view, undistracted by the life of the

*The graceful twin spires of Quimper's medieval cathedral, which dominate the city, were built as recently as the nineteenth century. The River Odet runs between the buildings in the foreground.*

*Part of Quimper's medieval town wall, built originally to defend the bishop's domain, which extended round the cathedral.*

*Next door to Quimper cathedral is the magnificent renaissance Bishop's Palace, now a museum of Breton life and culture.*

town swarming outside. The close itself is a delightful spot; it is reached through a little cloister just south of the cathedral, and this quiet oasis, shaded by a large weeping willow, forms an outdoor anteroom to the Musée Breton. This museum of Breton life and culture, rich in local pottery, traditional furniture and nineteenth-century costume, is housed in a splendid stone renaissance building, which was once the bishop's palace and has a magnificently wide spiral staircase. Costumes, feasting peasants and townscape

*The great west doorway of Quimper Cathedral. It was badly damaged during the Revolution, when most of its statues were destroyed.*

come together in my favourite painting of long-vanished Brittany – the bustling, Breughel-like *Le Champ de Foire à Quimper*, painted by Olivier Perrin at the beginning of the nineteenth century.

North of the cathedral, the little Place de Laënnec is the scene of a lively open-air market. It is named after René Laënnec, inventor of the stethoscope, who was born in Quimper in 1781. His bronze statue sits on a large tome entitled *Auscultation*, which means, according to the *Oxford English Dictionary*, 'the action of listening, with ear or stethoscope, to the sound of the movement of heart, lungs, or other organs'. Across the square is Quimper's art gallery, the Musée des Beaux-Arts; its extensive collection includes works by Italian and Dutch masters, and fine nineteenth-century paintings of the Breton scene by Eugène Boudin (*Le Port de*

*Quimper*) and Paul Sérusier, a disciple of Gauguin, whose powerful *La Vieille de Pouldu* shows an ageless peasant figure leaning on the haft of a mattock, with a rocky seascape behind. (Like the Musée Breton, the Beaux-Arts is at present being enlarged and is due to reopen towards the end of 1992.)

A section of the gallery is devoted to the life and work of Max Jacob, the poet and artist, who was born in Quimper in 1876. In his twenties he went to Paris, where he met Picasso, Apollinaire and other avant-garde artists, and established himself as their intellectual equal. His key work, a collection of surrealist prose poems called *Le Cornet à Dés* (*The Dicebox*) was published in 1916; it was followed in the 1920s by the *Poèmes de Morven le Gaëlique*, which are far simpler and hark back to Jacob's Quimper childhood. Arrested as a Jew by the Gestapo in February 1944, he was taken to the concentration camp at Drancy, in north-east Paris, where he died a few weeks later. In 1976 the Quimpérois honoured the centenary of his birth by renaming the main bridge across the Odet the Pont Max Jacob.

Quimper's medieval streets, several of them pedestrianized, lie west and north of the cathedral. The most famous of them, the Rue Kéréon, is lined with the superb houses, stone-built on the ground floor and half-timbered above, that are the city's pride. Worth hunting out in the Rue du Guéodet nearby is an ancient house with four grotesque groups of carved stone figures holding up the main beam of the façade. A little way up the hill is the prettiest square in Quimper, the Place au Beurre, which used to be called by the even more delightful name of Place au Beurre en Pot.

These old streets lay within the domain of the bishop, in the walled town or Ville Close, whose western limit was defined by the little River Steïr. Across the river was secular Quimper, the duke's

*A painted wooden statue of a Breton peasant in traditional costume enlivens a medieval house front in the Rue Kéréon.*

domain or Terre au Duc, perpetuated in a square of the same name. As in the Ville Close, the Middle Ages live on in the street names, such as the Venelle du Poivre and the Venelle du Pain Cuit (Pepper Lane and Bread Lane).

The oldest part of Quimper lies on the other side of the Odet, ten minutes' walk away below Mont Frugy, in the backwater of Locmaria. In Roman times Locmaria was called Aquilonia, and it seems probable that this was the original seat of the bishopric. It has one of Brittany's most beautiful romanesque churches, dedicated to the Virgin (the name Locmaria means 'Mary's Place'). Formerly a priory church, it is a massively austere eleventh-century building, with a superb west door and sturdy cruciform nave columns. On its south side is a quiet little flower-filled cloister, which looks medieval but is in fact seventeenth-century.

*The Rue Kéréon, the most famous of Quimper's medieval streets. The great gothic west front of the cathedral looms in the background.*

*Though mainly a renaissance building, Locronan church retains a distinctly Breton gothic character in details like this little window on the north side (see p. 124).*

A few steps from the church is the pottery which has carried the name of Quimper round the world. Here you can join a conducted tour to watch potters sitting at their wheels to shape cups, plates and pots of every description, and artists hard at work on the traditional Quimper designs of peasants and floral motifs that date back a century or more. Pottery has been made at Locmaria since Roman times, as it was ideally placed for the craft: near by were plentiful supplies of suitable clay and wood for the kilns, while the Odet gave easy access to the outside world for exporting the finished product. Today's enterprise dates its beginnings back to 1690, when Jean-Baptiste Bousquet, a businessman from Marseilles, took over the *poterie* run by Locmaria Priory and turned it into a *faïencerie* producing glazed majolica-style ware. After his death in 1708, the pottery passed from father to son, or son-in-law. The most notable figure was Pierre Clement Caussy, author of a *Traité de la Faïence* published in 1747, which not only gives the secrets of the potter's craft but is also a handbook on running a factory in an eighteenth-century paternalistic way.

The typical Quimper ware on which the modern products are based is that of the nineteenth century, the period of the so-called 'Grande Maison', distinguished by the maker's mark HB. This stands for Hubaudière-Bousquet, which unites the names of the founder of the pottery and of Caussy's daughter Marie-Elisabeth, who married Antoine de la Hubaudière and carried on under her married name (with an interlude during the Revolution when she reverted to 'Citoyenne Caussy') after her husband was guillotined in 1793. The last member of the family was killed in action in 1915. Examples of Quimper ware of all periods can be seen in the museum at the factory.

The Place de la Résistance, immediately below Mont Frugy, is the setting for the annual Festival de Cornouaille, a week-long celebration of Breton-ness held each July. Performers come from all over Brittany to vie with one another in the splendour of their regional costumes, the agility of their folk-dancing, and the virtuosity of their musicianship on *binious* (bagpipes), *bombardes* (Breton oboes), drums, accordions and other outdoor instruments. The festival ends with a grand riverside firework display and a *fest-noz* (night celebration), in which thousands of Quimpérois join hands to dance the Breton gavotte under the trees and through the ancient streets of the town, restoring their flagging energies with crêpes and cider.

Like other major Breton festivals, this one is as much a display of Celtic solidarity as an opportunity for general enjoyment: Irish, Scots and other European Celtic groups take part, and Breton singers like Alan Stivell use all the resources of modern rock and electronic music to lament the passing of former national glories, or look to some more hopeful future.

From Quimper, take the D34 south to the seaside resort of Bénodet, at the mouth of the Odet river (the meaning of its name, Ben-Odet). With its two fine beaches it is one of Finistère's most popular holiday centres, and has been a favourite with British holiday-makers since the nineteenth century. It is the starting-point for river trips up the beautiful Odet valley, which otherwise remains largely invisible between steep tree-covered banks. Resort and river inspired a poem by Apollinaire, who amidst the horrors of World War I wrote nostalgically of the 'blue-sailed fishing boats of Bénodet', and the river 'sweeter than the sound of its name' ('*L'Odet plus douce encore que ne sonne son nom.*')

Head east on the D44 and turn on to the cul-de-sac D45, which ends at the much smaller and more exclusive resort of Beg-Meil, where nineteenth-century villas perch on the end of a promontory, looking towards Concarneau across the Baie de la Forêt. Like the beeches on Quimper's Mont Frugy, most of the glorious pine trees which were once such a feature of Beg-Meil were shattered in the hurricane of October 1987. It will take thirty or forty years before the saplings planted to replace them reach maturity, and Beg-Meil regains the seclusion it had when Proust stayed there a century ago.

Back on the main coast road, continue round to Concarneau through the villages of Fouesnant and La Forêt-Fouesnant. There is little evidence of any natural forest today; but this is orchard country, with apple trees that are said to produce the best cider in Brittany. Fouesnant holds its Fête des Pommiers ('Apple-Tree Festival') on the first Sunday after July 14, when the locals parade in their colourful traditional costume (*Giz Fwen*, 'Costume of Fouesnant').

Concarneau has three distinct personalities: the seaside resort of sandy beaches facing across the bay to Beg-Meil; the tuna-fishing port – the most important in France – with its harbour buildings, boatyards and canning factories; and the medieval walled town, or Ville Close, which is the Concarneau that visitors come to see. Built on a small crescent-shaped island and linked to the mainland by a narrow causeway, it preserves the medieval illusion complete, provided you shut your eyes to the modern bustle all around. Concarneau's Breton name is Konk-Kernev, the 'Creek of Cornouaille' – a creek that has made it an important port since at least the thirteenth century. Its fortifi-cations were mainly laid out by Vauban (1633–1707), Louis XIV's chief military engineer.

There is not much to do in the Ville Close except walk round the ramparts (the authorities levy a charge, which plenty of people seem willing to pay), eat crêpes, buy curios, and visit the small but fascinating fishing museum, which displays a number of fishing-boats, together with tackle of all sorts, navigational instruments, and historic paintings and photographs. Every August Concarneau holds its Fête des Filets Bleus ('Festival of the Blue Nets'), originally a simple festival for blessing the nets to guarantee success in the forthcoming fishing season, but now expanded into a five-day folk jamboree. While it lasts, nets are hung along the causeway between the mainland and the Ville Close, while the crowds cram shoulder to shoul-der along the single narrow main street.

Concarneau was well known to Paul Gauguin (1848–1903), who got into a brawl there when he was living and painting at Pont-Aven, 14 kilometres down the coast. In May 1894 he visited the Ville Close with his mistress, known as 'Anna the Javanese', who added to her exotic appearance by carrying a tame monkey on her shoulder. The local children began to taunt her, and finally started throwing stones. A group of sailors emerged from a café, and a full-scale fight began. Gauguin describes in a letter how he knocked out a ship's pilot, was attacked by fifteen sailors, broke his leg in a pothole, and had to be carried back to Pont-Aven. To round off the story, Anna the Javanese rifled his Paris studio while he was away and walked off with the proceeds.

The spirit of Gauguin is everywhere in Pont-Aven, though oddly enough you will not see any of his paintings on permanent display there. The square beside the bridge is named after him, and you can follow his favourite walk beside the fast-flowing Aven river under the trees of the Bois d'Amour – most of them battered into a tangle of splintered trunks and broken branches by the hurricane of October 1987. When Gauguin first came to Pont-Aven in 1886, it was

a quiet backwater where artists could sit in the road for a drink, a game of cards and a chat; but nowadays it can take you ten minutes to cross the road as the juggernauts thunder down towards the river, and the summer tourist traffic crawls along nose-to-tail.

By the time Gauguin arrived there, it was already well established as an artists' mecca. Randolph Caldecott, the Victorian illustrator of *John Gilpin* and other children's books, drew and described it in the 1870s:

> On approaching Pont-Aven the traveller notices a curious noise rising from the ground and from the woods around him. It is the flickering of the paint brushes on the canvases of the hardworking painters who come into view on leafy nooks and shady corners. These artists go not far from the town where is cider, billiards and tobacco.

And he comments on the readiness of the local peasants to sit as artists' models for a franc a day, except at harvest time, when the fishermen lounging on the quayside below the bridge were a better bet.

After only a few months in Pont-Aven, Gauguin was the acknowledged leader of a group of artists living in the Pension Gloanec. As he wrote in a letter to his wife: 'I'm working here a lot, and quite successfully. I'm respected as the ablest painter at Pont-Aven, though I don't get a sou richer.' The Breton scenery and people provided the inspiration for his best work for almost five years, broken by two forays away from Brittany — the first in 1887 to Central America, and the second in 1888 to Arles, where he spent two months painting with Vincent Van Gogh, culminating in the scandal when Van Gogh cut off his own ear with a razor.

At Pont-Aven, Gauguin's leading disciples were Paul Sérusier and Emile Bernard (1868–1941). Sérusier coined the name 'Nabis' (from a Hebrew word meaning 'prophet') to describe the group of young artists that

*The yellow-painted wooden figure of Christ in Trémalo chapel, on a hill above Pont-Aven, inspired Gauguin to paint his* Christ Jaune.

adopted the new ideas of 'Synthetism', which juxtaposed violently contrasting colours, as opposed to the Impressionists' gentler intermingling of tones. Gauguin learnt in turn from his disciples: it was after seeing a painting by Bernard that he painted his great *The Vision after the Sermon*, now in the National Gallery of Scotland, Edinburgh. In this he abandoned conventional perspective, contrasting the coiffed audience of peasant women with the small figures of Jacob and the Angel wrestling on a brilliant red field. Gauguin offered this masterpiece as a gift to the priest of a neighbouring village, who turned it down on the grounds that his parishioners would not understand it. Exhibitions of works by artists of the Pont-Aven school from Gauguin's time to the present, or thereabouts, are held in summer at the Hôtel de Ville.

*The medieval walled town (Ville Close) of Concarneau, built on a small island linked to the mainland by a causeway.*

111

*St Luke writes his gospel inside the main entrance of the Eglise Sainte-Croix, Quimperlé's romanesque church.*

Do not leave Pont-Aven without driving (or preferably walking up the clearly marked path) to the chapel of Trémalo, tucked away high above the town between farm buildings and an avenue of beech trees. It is a simple stone building, with a low-pitched shingled roof sweeping almost to the ground, and a tiny open belfry, reached by steps cut in the gable end. Inside it is better preserved than most of these remote chapels; its frieze of grotesque carved faces at beam level are brightly painted, as are the grinning monsters whose jaws grip the end of each beam.

One treasure makes it unique in Brittany: the painted wooden figure of Christ on the cross, with arms stretched stiffly out and head downcast, which inspired Gauguin to paint one of the greatest of all his pictures, the *Christ Jaune* (now in the Albright-Knox Art Gallery, Buffalo). I first came to Trémalo one hot summer afternoon, with a postcard of the Yellow Christ for comparison, and felt a shock of recognition at seeing the original set high on the wall. Gauguin has captured the sinewy strength of the carving, bringing it out of the chapel and into the undulating folds of the Breton countryside. Behind the emaciated figure a handful of slate-roofed cottages nestle among the red-brown of the autumn trees; while the three Marys at the foot of the cross are Breton peasant women.

From Ponnt-Aven, the Gauguin trail leads eastwards to the small resort of Le Pouldu, at the mouth of the Laïta river. The road (D24) crosses the muddy Bélon estuary, one of Brittany's prime areas for growing oysters, known simply as Bélons, which you can sample in the town of Riec-sur-Bélon, or at roadside stalls offering *dégustations* to the passer-by. Gauguin moved to Le Pouldu in 1889, finding that Pont-Aven had become too crowded and sophisticated for his liking. It has grown a certain amount since then, but is still little more than a seaside village with a few large hotels; one of them, the Hôtel de la Plage, is said to be on the site of the *pension* where Gauguin stayed. In a letter to Emile Bernard he describes his summer activity – or inactivity – at Le Pouldu: 'I walk about like a savage with long hair and do nothing at all; I've not even got my paints or palette. I've made some arrows and I practise shooting them on the sand, as though I was in Buffalo Bill country.'

In 1895 Gauguin left Europe for good, spending the last eight years of his life first on Tahiti, then on the Marquesas islands, where he painted the powerful scenes of South Seas life on which his international reputation rests. In May 1903 he died of a heart attack shortly before his 55th birthday, in dire poverty, ravaged by syphilis, and mourned by the islanders among whom he lived. On his easel was the painting *A Breton Village Under Snow* (now in the Louvre). Although it is sometimes said to be his last work, it is more likely that he had brought it from Europe as a nostalgic reminder of his years in far-off Brittany. As a final irony, when his few effects were auctioned off, it was displayed upside down and sold as a picture of Niagara Falls.

The road north from Le Pouldu to Quimperlé (D49) runs through the Forêt de Carnoët, one of the few extensive stretches of woodland in south Finistère.. Now a state forest, mainly planted with beech and oak, it was once the lair of the legendary Breton Bluebeard, Comorrus, a sixth-century count of Cornouaille, who married a succession of wives and murdered them when they became pregnant. The last of them, Triphine, daughter of Waroch, Count of Vannes, had her head cut off by Comorrus, but was brought back to life by Gildas, the locality's leading saint, who replaced it on her shoulders. In due course she gave birth to a son, Trémeur, who was taught by Gildas and became a saint in his turn. In another version of the tale, it was Trémeur who was decapitated by Comorrus; whatever the truth behind the legends, his brutality must have been exceptional even in that bloodthirsty age.

From the trees of Carnoët you emerge at Quimperlé's stone quayside. The name of this delightful town derives, like that of Quimper, from the Breton Kemper, meaning 'river junction'; Quimperlé is an abbreviation for 'Quimper-Ellé', and the rivers that join there are the Ellé and the Isole, which meet in the heart of the town and flow south to the sea, under the new joint name of the Laïta. According to an old saying, 'If Quimper is the smile of Cornouaille, then Quimperlé is its kiss' – local patriotism perhaps, but not unjustified. Quimperlé consists of the old lower town, the Ville Basse, built where the rivers meet, and the more recent Ville Haute, on the hill in the direction of Pont-Aven, and reached by steep flights of steps from river level.

The town's chief glory is its romanesque abbey church, the Eglise Sainte-Croix, modelled on the Church of the Holy Sepulchre in Jerusalem. It was built in 1083 and heavily restored in the nineteenth century, after the belfry collapsed. In contrast to the angular severity of later gothic churches, everything about Sainte-Croix is gently rounded – round overall plan, round central tower, rounded apses at east, north and south, rounded roofs over the different sections. The only right angles are at the main west entrance, inside which is a spectacular stone renaissance screen depicting Christ in Majesty and the Four Evangelists.

*Adam and Eve carved on the brilliantly painted fifteenth-century rood screen in Saint-Fiacre chapel, near Le Faouët.*

Behind Sainte-Croix are several massively timbered medieval houses, notably the so-called Maison des Archers. The main church of the Ville Haute across the river, Notre Dame de l'Assomption, is a big gothic building with a thirteenth-century nave and fifteenth-century choir; its square tower no longer has its spire, as during the Revolution the lead covering was stripped off and turned into bullets.

Quimperlé was the birthplace of Vicomte Hersart de la Villemarqué, the leading nineteenth-century literary pioneer of the Breton revival. In 1838 he published the *Barzaz-Breiz* (*Songs of Brittany*), a collection of about eighty Breton poems of varying length and degrees of realism – battle scenes from the time of King Arthur to the eighteenth century, legends of saints and Druids, vignettes of peasant life from birth to death, lyrical descriptions of the countryside. It was the first

book to make the outside world realize that the Bretons had their own literature. Even the sophisticated Parisians were astonished: George Sand, with typical Romantic hyperbole, called the poems 'greater than the *Iliad*, more complete, more beautiful, more perfect than any masterpiece that has issued from the human brain'.

Though the *Barzaz-Breiz* looks like the life's work of an elderly scholar, La Villemarqué was only 23 when it was published. The rest of his long life was devoted to spreading the gospel of Breton language and literature. He died in 1895, having lived for nearly all his life on the family estate outside Quimperlé.

From Quimperlé, the D790 leads north towards Le Faouët, across gently undulating countryside. Just south of the town, in the village of Saint-Fiacre, is a hidden church treasure that is astonishing even by Breton standards. Saint-Fiacre's triple-spired chapel faces on to a wide green, and is unexpectedly large and elaborate for so small a place. Inside is a carved and painted rood-screen that glows like a jewelled casket in the building's gloom. Dating from 1480, when the chapel was built, it is surmounted by a lifelike and emaciated figure of the crucified Christ, above the Virgin, St John, and Adam and Eve. At the foot of each carved pendant, an angel swallow-dives gracefully into space on painted wings. Round the back, the Seven Deadly Sins are paraded: Sloth is a pair of musicians playing the Breton oboe and bagpipe; Theft is a peasant stealing fruit; while Greed is another peasant vomiting a fox from his mouth. ('*Il a trop bu de schnapps*' the chapel's *gardien* told us, for the benefit of German visitors.)

The highlight of the screen – or at least, the part the *gardien* was most proud of – is the Chaucer-like scene showing a fox disguised as a clergyman. He preaches from a pulpit to a group of hens, but (unlike Chaucer's Chanticleer) they are not taken in; they jump on his back and peck him furiously, while a cock tugs him by the nose, and a duck pulls on a back paw. We know the name of the artist-carver, Olivier Loërgan: has he perhaps left his self-portrait in the bearded face that peers at us round a curtain from the screen's top left-hand corner?

There is not much to see in Le Faouët itself, apart from its remarkable sixteenth-century covered market, 50m long by 20m wide, with massive wooden uprights and a sweeping roof supported by gigantic beams. A little way north of the town is another outstanding chapel, which both complements Saint-Fiacre and is in total contrast to it. The chapel of Sainte-Barbe (St Barbara) is a couple of kilometres along a back road, on a stretch of rolling heathland, and above a romantically wooded valley which drops steeply down to the Ellé river. Because of the sloping site, the building complex is on different levels. At the top is the *gardien*'s house, and just below it an open belfry, with a bell which you can ring to gain heaven's blessing. From the belfry, a grand double flight of balustraded steps, wide enough for processions, leads down to the chapel. Built around 1500 in Flamboyant gothic style, the chapel itself is long and narrow, due to the awkward ledge on which it stands. Its entrance front is enlivened by a series of enormous projecting gargoyles.

Inside there is little of interest, apart from a battered-looking wooden gallery carved with angels holding shields. The effigy of St Barbara is below the side altar; in Brittany she used to be invoked against storms, as in the doggerel rhyme:

> *Ste Barbe, Ste Claire,*
> *Préservez-moi du tonnerre*
> *Et du feu de l'enfer.*

> ('St Barbara and St Clare,
> Save me from thunder
> And the fires of hell'.)

Legend has it that the chapel was built by a local nobleman in thanksgiving after he escaped from a particularly violent storm.

---

*The sixteenth-century chapel of Sainte-Barbe, near Le Faouët, is almost hidden by the rocky slope on which it stands.*

To the right of the chapel, across a bridge, is a small oratory on a rocky outcrop. Fixed in the walls all round it are iron rings, where pilgrims swung themselves from hand to hand over the drop, for the good of their souls though at risk to their lives; if a convict succeeded in completing the circuit, he won his pardon. As a final example of Sainte-Barbe's accumulation of old wives' tales, the eighteenth-century fountain nearby used to be visited by local girls in search of a husband. They would throw a pin in the water: if it floated, they would be married within the year; if it sank, their turn had not yet come.

From Le Faouët, head north-west along the D769 to Gourin, a hard-working country town with no pretensions to beauty. It is a busy centre for the region's agricultural produce, and is also the capital of the Montagnes Noires, Brittany's 'Black Mountains', which are a good deal less bleak (and no more black) than the Monts d'Arrée to the north. They are shared between the three *départements* of Morbihan, Finistère and Côtes-d'Armor, and for all their small size form a definite barrier between the hill country to the north and the gentler farmland of southern Finistère.

A switchback road from Gourin to Châteauneuf-du-Faou (D117) winds inconsequentially for 20 kilometres, giving tremendous views northwards towards the Monts d'Arrée. Soon after Gourin, it passes directly below the highest crag of the Montagnes Noires, the 326m Roc de Toullaëron; a footpath on the right of the road leads up to the summit. Down a side road in the village of Spézet, at roughly the half-way point, is the pretty chapel of Notre Dame du Crann, a modest building with a neat little renaissance bell-tower decorated with winged heads of the winds puffing out their cheeks. Inside are rustic painted altar-panels and some colourful sixteenth-century stained glass. Across the road is a good example of a small rustic calvary.

Châteauneuf-du-Faou is an unpretentious town surrounded by hills. It stands on a ridge above the Aulne, which here forms part of the Nantes-Brest Canal, and flows wide and deep. The tree-clad slopes that fall away to the river below the town are said to be haunted by the ghostly mounted squadrons of King Arthur, who patrol the Montagnes Noires whenever Brittany is threatened by war. I shall always have affectionate memories of Châteauneuf, as some years ago I had the luck to be there during the annual *pardon* of Notre Dame des Portes, typical of the hundreds of local *pardons* held each year. Notre Dame chapel, where it takes place on the last weekend but one in August, is set high among the trees above the Aulne; though the present spiky gothic building is mainly nineteenth-century, it retains its original fifteenth-century porch.

Late on the Saturday evening we joined the candlelit procession as it emerged from the chapel door into the warm summer night. The faithful of Châteauneuf, carrying hundreds of flickering candles, were followed by white-robed clerics and choir, and then by the gold-crowned effigies of the Virgin and Child, carried by six men of the parish aged over fifty. For half an hour or so the procession wended through the town, up to the parish church with its memorial to 43 men of Châteauneuf shot by the Nazis, past shops and the town fountain, then down again to the chapel. At the end, the whole procession chanted a Breton hymn to Notre Dame des Portes: *Itron Varia ar Porziou, Klevit mouez ho pugale* ('Our Lady of the Gates, Hear the voices of your children'). Back at the chapel, the Virgin was returned to the brilliantly lit interior until the following day.

On Sunday morning there was a high mass; and in the afternon an open-air service was held in front of the chapel, with the congregation on seats up by the altar, or sprawled on the grass. Châteauneuf-du-Faou was out in force, from the smallest babies to old ladies in the tight local *coiffe*, holding umbrellas to keep off the heat of the sun. Then the procession was repeated, this time with ten women of the parish carrying the Virgin and Child. Finally the priest thanked the bishop

*A lock-keeper's cottage at Châteauneuf-du-Faou, on the River Aulne, at this point part of the Nantes-Brest Canal.*

and blessed the congregation; the Virgin and Child were placed by the altar for another year; and the chapel bells clanged out across the Aulne.

From Châteauneuf, drive 14 kilometres west to Pleyben. This little town, spacious in feeling despite its small size, has the grandest of all the parish closes, sited a good deal south of the cluster of *enclos* described in the previous chapter. The large and sumptuous church is immediately striking for its two towers, one fifteenth-century gothic with a pierced stone belfry cage, and the other in sixteenth-century renaissance style, four-square and topped by a large domed turret with four little turrets on the corners. Outside is a curious detached eighteenth-century sacristy, all curved domes and rounded apses. Inside, the church is brilliant with painted reredoses, carved wall-plates below the star-spangled ceilings, and statues of saints. At the west end is a grand organ gallery.

St Germain (Germanus), to whom the church is dedicated, is not the usual parochial Breton saint. He was born in Auxerre, south-east of Paris, in about 380, studied law in Rome and returned home to a successful legal career. Famous for his piety as well as his learning, he was elected bishop of Auxerre, though he had never been ordained. But at the age of about forty he gave away his possessions, left his wife and retired from the world, wearing rags and living on a starvation diet of ashes and dry barley bread. His religious powers were said to enable him to exorcize demons, free prisoners by making their manacles and prison bars break of their own accord, and even bring a dead youth back to life. In bygone Brittany St Germanus had a more prosaic reputation: he was called upon to cure children's stomach complaints.

Leaning against the wall at the west end of the church is a large cross, once wielded by a preacher twelve centuries later than Pleyben's patron saint. Painted with the legend 'Mission 1676', it was carried through Brittany by the Jesuit Père Julien Maunoir. One of the leaders of the seventeenth-century Catholic revival in Brittany, Maunoir tramped the countryside for half a century, preaching hell-fire to the peasantry. Missions like this continued until after World War II.

Pleyben has no triumphal arch; instead, on the west side of the close, near the ossuary, is a small arched gateway known as the Gate of Death (Porz ar Maro), through which coffins were carried. The large calvary, cruciform in plan, is extremely fine; it was probably begun about 1550 and completed a century later. Among its superb carvings is a realistic Last Supper, so little worn that even the food can be made out – a sucking-pig, fruit, a pie. The sculptor, Yves Ozanne, of Brest, has signed it along the lower stretcher, calling himself 'ARCHETECTE' (sic); perhaps he designed the whole ensemble, as well as carving the figures. The women at the foot of the cross have tears running down their cheeks, a dignified Pontius Pilate wears a turban, and the mouth of Hell gapes menacingly.

Continue west along the N164 to Châteaulin, a quiet little town on the Aulne, with tree-shaded riverside walks. The Aulne is a salmon-fishing river, and the fish appears on the town's coat-of-arms. In earlier centuries the salmon run was so vast that local farm-workers stipulated in their contracts that they would not eat salmon more than three times a week. After a decline since World War II, salmon numbers are again on the increase.

The road west from Châteaulin (D887) climbs steeply from the Aulne, to give wide views over Douarnenez Bay on the left, and the heather-covered dome of Menez-Hom, 330m high, on the right. Menez-Hom guards the Crozon Peninsula, and is protected by the conservation umbrella of the Parc Naturel Régional d'Armorique. Unlike Menez-Bré and Montagne Saint-Michel it has no chapel on its summit; but its views in every direction are far more extensive than theirs. Last time I went up there microlight aircraft were buzzing like hornets above the parked cars and coaches. During World War II the Germans fortified Menez-Hom as part of the defences of Brest, and you still stumble over traces of concrete emplacements among the gorse.

---

*The impressive calvary at Pleyben, whose carvings include a realistic Last Supper showing details of the meal.*

A kilometre or so before the turn up to Menez-Hom is the chapel of Sainte-Marie du Menez-Hom, in the hamlet of the same name. Gothic overall but rebuilt about 1670, it has a fanciful renaissance tower; in front of it is a worn calvary which shows Mary kneeling at the foot of the cross. Inside it has an elaborate reredos, painted statues of John the Baptist, Peter, Paul and other saints, and superb wooden decorative carvings; but as in so many Breton chapels, these treasures are suffering severely from the effects of damp, woodworm and general neglect. The chapel's state is not improved by the fact that many of the slates are off the roof, and the holes are covered in plastic. The *gardienne* told me that money for repairs had been promised years ago, but had not yet appeared.

The chapel played its part in World War II, when eighteen British and American airmen, shot down over Brittany, hid for weeks in a room at the back. The *gardienne* told me that her brother and a friend looked after them, taking turns at keeping guard and bringing them food; they eventually escaped to England by boat, some from Camaret and some from Brest. In those days Menez-Hom must have been at the back of beyond; but today, in summer at least, a seemingly endless stream of traffic hurtles past the chapel on its way to the Crozon resorts.

Continue west along the peninsula, turning north after 8 kilometres for Argol, worth a stop for its small parish close. The church is sixteenth century, while the triumphal arch dates from 1659. Above the arch is a figure on horseback said to be King Gradlon. The churchyard is crammed with gravestones, many of them the hideous modern variety made of black polished granite.

Carrying on through Argol, cross the main road (D791), then head east along a back road (D60) to Landévennec. Standing on an enchanting little tree-covered peninsula that curls like a crooked finger into the estuary of the Aulne, Landévennec is famous for its ruined Benedictine abbey, founded around AD 600 by St Guénolé, who was Breton-born, as his parents had emigrated from Britain. Guénolé won a reputation as a miracle-worker from an early age: while still a novice, he healed the foot of a fellow-novice who had been bitten by a snake, and – less credibly – replaced his little sister's eye in its socket, after it had been pecked out and swallowed by an angry goose. He built his monastery after St Patrick appeared to him in a vision, on land granted to him by Gradlon, King of Ys, whom he had converted to Christianity.

The Normans destroyed the abbey in the tenth century, but it was soon rebuilt on a grander scale; the capitals of the romanesque church, decorated with interlaced leaf motifs, are said to show Irish influence. Destroyed a second time during the Revolution, Landévennec came to life again after 1950, when Benedictines returned and built a new abbey near by.

From Landévennec, return to the main road and head west for Camaret-sur-Mer, at the end of the peninsula. The road runs through the small town of Crozon, linked to the popular resort of Morgat, which has a wide, curving beach backed by hotels. Camaret is the only town of any consequence on the peninsula. It has a pretty harbour protected by a natural breakwater of shingle, the Sillon de Camaret, which gives the town its Breton name, Kameret, *kam* meaning curved, and *ero* meaning furrow or land turned up by the plough. Until fairly recently it was a leading lobster-fishing port, though the trade has now declined; the line of hulks gently decaying on the shingle below the harbour wall bears witness to past prosperity. Camaret still has a small and busy lobster fleet, but most of its money comes from its booming tourist trade; even in late September, it can be difficult to find a room there.

Despite its present peaceful somnolence, Camaret has had its warlike moments. In 1694 troops from an Anglo-Dutch invasion fleet landed on the Sillon to attack the town and were repulsed. In the course of the action, the top of the chapel belfry was knocked off by a cannon-ball, and has been left unrepaired ever since.

---

*Looking towards Douarnenez Bay from the slopes of Menez-Hom, the 330-metre-high hill that guards the approaches to the Crozon Peninsula.*

The chapel, built early in the sixteenth century, is dedicated to Notre Dame de Rocamadour; though you might be puzzled to find a Breton chapel bearing the name of a town in the Dordogne, there is a logical explanation. In the Middle Ages Rocamadour was a halting-place on the pilgrim route to Santiago de Compostela, in north-west Spain, and was itself a pilgrimage centre. Travellers returning home from Rocamadour would often make for Bordeaux or La Rochelle, and from there sail north round Brittany, calling at Camaret *en route*, and offering prayers for a safe return in the chapel. Our Lady of Rocamadour protected sailors in danger of shipwreck: hence the many *ex voto* ship models that hang in the chapel, placed there by sailors saved from drowning.

At the end of the Sillon, Camaret's harbour is guarded by the Tour Vauban. This small polygonal fortress, built in 1689, is quite unlike any other of Vauban's fortifications. It is now a nautical museum. Prominent among the old maps, charts and diving-gear is the nameplate of the *Torrey Canyon*, which broke up between Land's End and the Scillies in 1967, spilling thousands of tons of oil into the sea and polluting huge stretches of the Breton coast. Camaret's heroism in World War II is recalled by a model of a fishing smack with a proud if idiomatic inscription: 'Many allied airfighters, crashed in France during Second World War have been driven in Great Britain by the ship *Suzanne-Renée* and her valorious crew.' Perhaps the airmen from Sainte-Marie du Menez-Hom were among them.

Beyond Camaret the mighty Pointe de Penhir, central of the three prongs of the Crozon Peninsula, looms 70m above the rocky foreshore. On a clear day you can stand on Penhir and see a tremendous panoramic seascape, which takes in both the Pointe de Saint-Mathieu beyond the Rade de Brest, and the

*The blind St Hervé is led by a guide and dog in this sixteenth-century group carved in granite outside the chapel of Sainte-Anne-la-Palud, an important Breton pilgrimage centre.*

Pointe du Raz across Douarnenez Bay. Behind the car-park is a sombrely impressive granite monument to the Bretons who died in World War II, in the shape of a Cross of Lorraine.

Leaving the peninsula, you have to retrace the route back through Camaret and Crozon. Fork right on the D887 5 kilometres east of Crozon, and just beyond Telgruc-sur-Mer fork right again on to the minor road that hugs the coast of Douarnenez Bay. This is not a quick way of covering the ground; but it is a delightful up-and-down pottering kind of journey, often within sight of the sea, and a reminder of what driving in Brittany used to be like before the road-improvement programme of the past twenty years. Past splendid beaches like Pentrez-Plage, you come suddenly on

*The harbour of Camaret is protected by a natural breakwater, on which stand a sixteenth-century sailors' chapel and a small seventeenth-century fortress.*

the pilgrim chapel of Sainte-Anne-la-Palud ('St Anne of the Marshes'), whose spire appears ahead above the grassy dunes.

The big nineteenth-century chapel stands isolated on a broad sweep of grass, with dunes behind, and the waters of the bay stretching beyond. Apart from the ancient calvary in front of it, and a sixteenth-century statue of St Anne – mother of the Virgin Mary – inside, there is nothing particularly memorable about it. But it traces its origins back to King Gradlon and stands on the site of a far older chapel, which has been venerated for centuries. Each August one of Brittany's most important *pardons* is held there. The artist Charles Cottet has left a record of the *pardon* as it was a century ago in a fine painting in the Musée des Beaux-Arts in Rennes; and a generation earlier the Roscoff poet Tristan Corbière described it in his masterly poem 'La Rapsode Foraine' ('The Itinerant Ballad-singer').

When Corbière was writing in the years round 1870, a *pardon* was still the gathering-place not just for the healthy worshipper but for the sick, the mad and the maimed, who would attend in hope of a cure at best, or at least of a handout from the charitable. His poem paints a Brueghel-like picture of the faithful going round the chapel three times on their knees, of consumptives and epileptics, of a man with a growth that hangs on him like mistletoe on a tree, of a mother and daughter with St Vitus' Dance. As for the *rapsode* herself, she bellows out a ballad for a copper or two; if you give her some tobacco:

> *Tu verras dans sa face creuse*
> *Se creuser, comme dans du bois,*
> *Un sourire; et sa main galeuse*
> *Te faire un vrai signe de croix.*

('Her hollow cheeks will wrinkle into a smile, as though carved in wood, and her scabby hand will make you a true sign of the cross.')

From Sainte-Anne, drive inland through Plonévez-Porzay to the little stone-built town of Locronan. It is one of Finistère's main tourist attractions, and deservedly so, though its conservation has gone so far that it is more like a stage set than a living town. Its sixteenth- and seventeenth-century houses were built by merchants who grew rich from supplying sailcloth to the French fleet; today, spruce and flower-bedecked, they have been largely turned into craft workshops and salerooms for pottery, sculpture and woven materials.

Fronting the main square is the big fifteenth-century parish church, dedicated to the Irish monk St Ronan; unlike most Breton churches, which tend to be gloomy, it is flooded with light from enormous windows, and it is rare in having a stone-vaulted ceiling. A side chapel contains the empty tomb of the saint, with a fifteenth-century effigy on it, while the chief events of his life are depicted on medallions on the pulpit. In Locronan it is well worth exploring the steep little alleyways off the main street; down one of them, lined with low granite side-doors, is a beautiful little stone open-air washplace, where Locronan's housewives scrubbed their clothes in the sociable days before washing machines were invented.

Locronan has its own special *pardon*, known as the Grande Troménie, which takes place every six years on the third Sunday in July. The procession wends its way cross-country to the chapel at the top of the Montagne de Locronan east of the town, stopping at no fewer than 44 shrines along the way. In the intervening years Locronan holds a smaller celebration, the Petite Troménie.

No town could be a greater contrast to tourist Locronan than hardworking Douarnenez, 10 kilometres to the west. One of France's major fishing ports, it is built on a small peninsula, with the open waters of Douarnenez Bay on one side and the deep estuary of Port-Rhu, the old fishing-harbour, on the other. Its working centre has shifted from Port-Rhu to the Nouveau Port, built out into the bay, with massive storage areas and refrigerated warehouses. Across Port-Rhu is Douarnenez's lesser half, the resort of

*The elaborate west front of the fifteenth-century church at Locronan, a small town full of beautifully restored merchants' houses.*

Tréboul, which has its own little harbour for pleasure craft, and the best beaches of the neighbourhood.

The town's strange name has given rise to various conjectures about its origin. One is that it derives from Tutuarn Enez, the 'Island of Tutuarn', after a hermit who built himself a cell there in the sixth century. Or it may come from the Breton Douar Nevez, the 'New Land' that appeared when King Gradlon's city of Ys was swallowed up by the sea. Off the mouth of the estuary is the tree-covered Ile Tristan, a name which has links with yet another Celtic legend. Tristan, the lover of Isolde and hero of Wagner's opera, is said to have been given the island by King Mark, who had his palace at Douarnenez – though Cornishmen, and Wagner, set the scene not in Brittany but in Cornwall.

At the end of the sixteenth century the Ile Tristan was used as a stronghold by the villainous Guy Eder de La Fontenelle, the most savage of the guerrilla leaders produced by France's religious wars. Ostensibly fighting for the Ligue – the League of fanatical anti-Protestant Catholics – La Fontenelle soon abandoned any religious principles he may have had and turned his attention to murder and pillage. After devastating the inland region of Cornouaille, in 1595 he captured the Ile Tristan and made it his headquarters for sacking towns and villages all round the coast. His bloody career lasted until 1602, when he was captured, condemned to death and broken on the wheel in Paris.

In recent years Douarnenez has set up an outstanding maritime museum devoted to the wooden fishing-boats from which this coast once made its living. The Musée du Bateau, on Port-Rhu's long quayside, stands in an attractive waterside square called for some reason Place de l'Enfer ('Hell Square'). Housed in a converted sardine-canning factory, it has more than 200 small boats, of all shapes and sizes, and from many places and periods – fragments of 8000-year-old dugouts recovered from a Breton swamp, a Portuguese fishing-

*Fishing boats set out across the bay from Douarnenez, which is still one of France's main fishing harbours.*

boat whose curved shape might have come from an ancient Egyptian papyrus, a boat from the shallows of the Gulf of Morbihan known as a *sinago*, with a pair of russet lateen sails like those of an Arab dhow. Though the collection consists mainly of fishing-boats, there are frivolous outsiders, like a racing skiff, and a vintage speedboat or two.

Leave Douarnenez by the D765 and make for Pont-Croix, 20 kilometres to the west. But stop on the way in the village of Confort-Meilars to look inside the sixteenth-century church for its extraordinary carillon-wheel, consisting of a wooden wheel with twelve small bells, tuned to different notes and hung round the perimeter. The *gardienne* will let you turn the wheel yourself: the resulting jangle has a jazzy beat. The carillon is said to date from the foundation of the church, and was believed to have the power of curing speech defects when rung above the heads of stammering or mute children. Confort's splendid sixteenth-century east window is in the form of a Jesse Tree, with panels showing such obscure sages as Joram, Abiam, Asa and Joas. The wall-plates above the carillon are carved with all sorts of strange figures, including the heads of a Chinese mandarin, and a couple of Incas.

Pont-Croix is a dozy little medieval town of steep cobbled streets leading down to the Goyen river. It was one of the towns pillaged in the 1590s by La Fontenelle. The huge church, part romanesque, part gothic, has a giant tower, with a spire almost 70m high, and an outsize Flamboyant gothic porch at the west end. Inside, the great nave pillars lean outwards from their base; in contrast to their grandeur, the light-hearted renaissance font is carved with cavorting cherubs.

From Pont-Croix, head north along country lanes for the coast road (D7) and the bird sanctuary of Cap Sizun. Reached down a side road near the village of Goulien, Cap Sizun is remote enough not to get overcrowded, even in midsummer. It was founded in 1958 by the Breton ornithologist Michel-Hervé Julien, after a slaughter of seabirds by tourists on an offshore island and in the face of a threat to build a road right along the coast, which fortunately never materialized. The

*Ancient fishing boats settle gently in the mud of the Goyen estuary near Audierne.*

mighty cliffs and deep inlets of this rocky coast provide ideal nesting-sites for kittiwakes, guillemots, cormorants, petrels and gulls of all sorts; the reserve is open from mid-March until the end of August, which takes in both the breeding season and the period when the young birds are being fed in the nest.

West of Cap Sizun, Cornouaille tapers away to Brittany's Land's End, the Pointe du Raz. The road leads down from the high ground to the Baie des Trépassés ('Bay of the Dead'), before climbing up again to the village of Lescoff and out to the Pointe. The bay is named after the souls who embarked there for the Celtic Isles of the Dead, somewhere far to the west, or, more likely, after the sailors who drowned in the treacherous currents swirling round the headland. It has a marvellous west-facing beach, and a large hotel, not quite so marvellous, but only to be expected in such a magnificent place. The actress Sarah Bernhardt

(1844–1923) used to come to the bay in the 1870s to sketch, and wrote nostalgically in her memoirs of a time when Brittany was 'not furrowed with roads; its green slopes were not dotted with small white villas; its inhabitants – the men – were not dressed in the abominable modern trousers, and the women did not wear miserable little hats with feathers'.

What the Divine Sarah would make of the Pointe du Raz today is not hard to guess (though she would no longer have to worry about feathered hats). It is now a tourist trap of vast car-parks, curio shops and cafés, with its turf worn away by the shoe-leather of hundreds of thousands of feet, not to mention the tyres of cars and motorbikes. A statue of Notre Dame des Naufrages ('Our Lady of Shipwrecks') stands on the headland above the jagged rocks of the Pointe, looking across the swift-flowing Raz de Sein (*raz* is the same word as the English 'race') to the Ile de Sein lying low on the horizon.

Rising little more than a metre above high tide – so low that the houses seem almost afloat – and surrounded by rocky reefs, Sein is one of the most mysterious of Brittany's offshore islands. It was the Druids' Isle of the Dead, and remained pagan until the seventeenth century, 1000 years after the conversion of the rest of Brittany. Its greatest historical moment came in June 1940, when every man of fighting age, 130 altogether, left Sein to join De Gaulle's Free French forces in England. Reviewing his first tiny contingent of 500 men, De Gaulle made the famous comment '*Sein est donc le quart de la France*' ('So Sein is one quarter of France'). If there is any truth in the theory of global warming, Sein will not be around much longer, as it will be one of the first places to disappear below the waves as the ice-caps melt.

The boat for Sein leaves from Audierne, 15 kilometres from the Pointe du Raz along the southern coast

*The substantial houses on the waterfront at Audierne date from the period of the town's prosperity as a leading tuna-fishing port.*

*A modern bronze statue in the square at Plozévet shows a pair of musicians playing the* bombarde *(Breton oboe) and* biniou *(bagpipe).*

road (D784). Audierne is a prosperous-looking fishing port with a fine sweep of waterfront houses, divided neatly in two by the estuary of the River Goyen. However, its prosperity is very much a thing of the past; once a leading tuna-fishing port, it now lives mainly from catching lobsters and crayfish, and from a booming tourist trade.

From Audierne, continue along the coast road to Plozévet. In the main square, across the road from the church, is a lifelike bronze group of the typical Breton musical *couple* of oboe and bagpipe, by the sculptor René Quillivic. The sixteenth-century church stands on sloping ground, which means that the west door is down a flight of six steps. Plozévet is the only church I know to have its own exclusive water-supply: the south (entrance) porch stands above a spring, and on either side are tanks full of water. No doubt when Brittany was converted to Christianity the church was built directly above a spring sacred to some Celtic water-spirit.

The World War II memorial beside Plozévet church is carved with a grieving mother wearing the tall *coiffe* typical of the Pays Bigouden – the name given to the area of Finistère that lies south-west of Quimper. Though its boundaries are imprecise, it extends south-wards from Plozévet to its own Land's End at the Pointe de Penmarc'h, and has its own small capital in the town of Pont-l'Abbé. The life of this windswept region of bright light and plain little villages has been immortalized by the Breton writer Pierre-Jakez Hélias, who was born shortly before World War I in the village of Pouldreuzic, 6 kilometres from Plozévet.

In his book *Le Cheval d'Orgeuil* (1975), Hélias chronicles the passing of his ancestral civilization without sentimentality and with a mosaic-like wealth of detail. He describes the unending toil of his parents in the fields round Pouldreuzic, the building, buying and selling of houses, the rich heritage of Breton tales and culture passed down to him by his grandfather. The 'Horse of Pride' from which the book takes its name was his grandfather's pride in those traditions – which, the young Hélias found, meant little or nothing in a school where a pupil caught speaking Breton rather than French was punished, and in a wider outside world where Paris rather than Pont-l'Abbé was the ultimate touchstone of life. Most of the cottages where Hélias and his friends grew up have fallen down or been made into second homes; he ends with a vision of a future (soon to be with us, if not already here) where the peasants have all moved to the cities, while their employers buy up the homesteads they have abandoned, and rediscover the joys of rusticity and unprocessed food.

*The Eckmühl lighthouse on the Pointe de Penmarc'h, at the southern tip of Cornouaille. The coast here is fringed by dangerous reefs.*

*The chapel of Languidou, near Plovan, built in the thirteenth century and wrecked during the Revolution.*

Just south of Pouldreuzic, outside the village of Plovan in an area of dunes and tidal pools, is the ruined chapel of Languidou. One of the high points of Breton medieval architecture, it was built about 1260, much altered in the fifteenth century, and wrecked during the Revolution, when many of its stones were taken to build a coastal strongpoint. Though its stained glass has long since disappeared, the intricate tracery of its rose window is still largely intact.

Back on the D2, turn right in Plonéour-Lanvern on to the D57, and make for the lonely chapel of Notre Dame de Tronoën. Standing on rolling dunes with the sea only a few hundred metres away, the chapel is a simple fifteenth-century gothic building typical of dozens throughout Brittany. But the calvary beside it, carved about 1465 and thought to be the oldest in Brittany, is altogether exceptional. Lichen-covered and gnawed for centuries by the strong sea wind off the Bay of Audierne, these carvings of the Last Supper and Crucifixion have never been restored. Among them is a bare-breasted Virgin suckling the infant Jesus; unlike such figures at La Martyre and elsewhere, this Virgin has escaped mutilation, saved no doubt by Tronoën's remoteness.

From Tronoën, the road twists and turns parallel to the sea, through the village of Saint-Guénolé, which has a small museum of prehistory, and out to the Pointe de Penmarc'h (pronounced 'Penmar'). Just before the Pointe, the roads passes one of the prettiest of all the Breton chapels, the delightfully named Notre Dame de la Joie, built on a small creek and a real seafarer's church. The Pointe de Penmarc'h is not much of a headland, though it has a lighthouse to warn ships off the reefs that stretch far out to sea at low tide. Offshore is a seaweed-festooned rock shaped like the head *(pen)* of a horse *(marc'h)*, perhaps the rock from which the Pointe gets its name.

Penmarc'h village lies a little way inland; though today it basks in an atmosphere of sleepy decay, it was once one of Brittany's main harbour towns, and its big Flamboyant gothic church harks back to wealthier times. In 1595 the thugs under the command of La Fontenelle sacked the town, shut 3000 people in the church and slaughtered them within its walls. After such horrors, Penmarc'h never fully recovered its former prosperity.

From Penmarc'h, head east along the D53 to Loctudy. This small family resort, which looks across an island-studded estuary, has one of Brittany's few romanesque churches, built in the early twelfth century but concealed behind an eighteenth-century façade. It gets its name from St Tudy, who is said to have built a hermitage here in the fifth century, after sailing over from Britain. The interior columns, crammed closely together, have ornate capitals, mainly in a crude imitation of the classical Corinthian style, but some carved with curious stylized human faces; while several of their bases are carved with naked figures of men and women.

Drive next to Pont-l'Abbé, a quiet little riverside town which gets its name from a bridge built in the

Middle Ages by the abbots of Loctudy. The medieval castle which dominates the main square is both the town hall and a museum, the Musée Bigouden, devoted to the region's furniture and costumes. The tall Bigouden *coiffe*, still worn by a few elderly women, grew to its present impressive size (32cm is now the standard height) during the early decades of this century. Rumour has it that the roofs of Bigouden buses were raised to allow for the *coiffe*, and its view-blocking height no doubt caused a good deal of ill-feeling in the days when women wore it to the cinema.

The main road back to Quimper (D785) keeps to the high ground, but you can branch off it a few kilometres north of Pont-l'Abbé and take the far prettier – and less crowded – minor road along the Odet river.

*Inside Loctudy's romanesque church. The capitals and bases of the close-packed columns are decorated with fanciful carvings.*

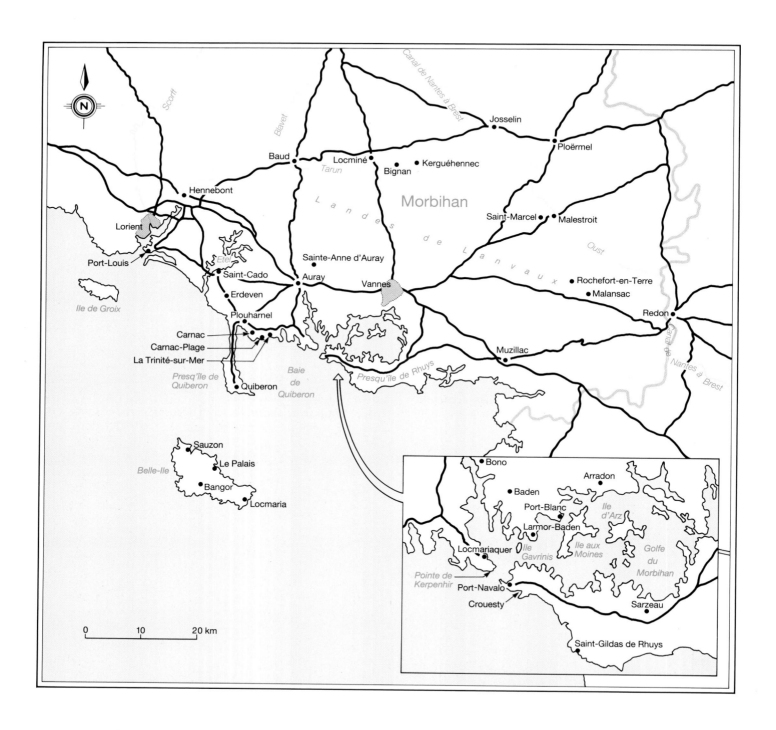

# 5
# The Gulf of Morbihan

*Vannes – Auray – Carnac – Quiberon – Belle-Ile – Lorient*

*Ile de Groix – Josselin – Ploërmel – Rhuys Peninsula*

The venerable city of Vannes stands at the head of the Gulf of Morbihan – the inland sea, studded with dozens of tree-covered islands, that is quite unlike any other part of Brittany. The administrative centre of the Morbihan *département*, it has achieved civic dignity without pomposity. In many ways it is comparable to Quimper, though everything – at least in the medieval part, called Intra-Muros ('within the walls', as at Saint-Malo) – is on a much smaller scale. Even the long stretch of medieval wall, complete with towers and machicolations, has been domesticated by a sweep of formal municipal gardening in the drained moat at its foot – a typically Breton combination of grey stone walls and brightly planted flower-beds, which is most people's first view of the town.

Vannes gets its name from the Veneti, a powerful Gaulish tribe conquered by Julius Caesar in 56 BC. Under the Romans, it was the starting-point for a network of roads radiating all over Brittany; and in the ninth century Nominoë, the first ruler of Brittany, proclaimed his country's independence here. Almost exactly 700 years later that same independence died at Vannes, when in 1532 the Etats of Brittany declared their wish to be united with France. For some years after

1675 Vannes was the centre of Breton administration, when Louis XIV moved the Etats there from Rennes.

Though there are several gates into the old town through the medieval wall, the best starting-point is down by the harbour, where there is plenty of parking space. Walk from the waterfront across the sober semi-circle of the Place Gambetta and through the Porte Saint-Vincent, an elegant renaissance gateway on an ancient site. It gets its name from St Vincent Ferrier, Vannes' patron saint, whose statue, with his right hand raised in blessing, stands in a niche above the entrance. It is strange to find a Spaniard rather than a Breton as the patron saint of one of Brittany's major towns; but he preached at Vannes and died there, and his tomb and reliquary are in the cathedral.

The Place Valencia, in the heart of medieval Vannes, commemorates the Spanish town where St Vincent was born in the 1350s. For decades he preached throughout Europe, reuniting the Roman Catholic church when it was in danger of being torn apart by schism. He arrived in Brittany in 1416 and spent some time at Nantes before moving on to Vannes, which he entered – Père Albert Le Grand tells us – *monté sur un meschant asne* ('riding on a bad-tempered donkey'). From

Vannes he travelled all over Brittany, preaching to 'great and small, wise men and fools'; but in 1419 he was taken mortally ill in the city and died after a short illness, in the presence of the Duchess of Brittany, and mourned by all around him. Père Albert describes the poetic miracle that accompanied his death:

> A great number of white butterflies of marvellous beauty were seen to flutter beside the window of his room, and they did not leave until he had rendered up his spirit. The pious believed that it was a flight of angels who, in the guise of these little creatures, waited for the release of his soul to escort it to eternal life.

The cathedral is at the top of the town, and is reached through narrow streets and small squares laid out in the haphazard, medieval way. The best of the half-timbered streets are now pedestrianized, which makes it easy, and safe, to stand back and study the old carvings on many of the houses. The most famous of them, on the corner of the Place Valencia and the Rue Noë, has been nicknamed 'Vannes and his Wife'; it is a cheerfully painted granite carving of a plump bourgeois couple, looking smugly down on the cafés and curio shops. Near by in the Rue Noë is the Château Gaillard, a magnificent medieval town house, home of Vannes' museum of prehistory. Run by the sonorously named Société Polymathique du Morbihan, it is crammed with stone tools, some going back 400,000 years, decorated pottery, turquoise necklaces, bronze swords and spears, and primitive coinage, from the palaeolithic to the Iron Age.

Walk up the Rue des Halles towards the Rue Saint-Salomon. On your right is the ancient covered market, known as La Cohue ('The Hubbub'), which runs through the entire block from the Rue des Halles to the square in front of the cathedral. Built in stages from the thirteenth century on, La Cohue consisted originally of the market on the ground floor and the Palais de Justice above. When the Etats moved to Vannes, the upper floor became the parliament building; and during the Revolution it was turned into a theatre, which remained in use until 1940. La Cohue has been restored and transformed into an excellent museum-cum-art gallery which combines the collections from the former art gallery (Beaux-Arts) and the local museum (Musée du Golfe). The conversion has been most imaginatively carried out, leaving the great medieval beams visible above the new glass-walled viewing spaces.

Pride of the permanent collection is a *Crucifixion* by Delacroix (1798–1963); but La Cohue is richer in scenes of Breton life than in major works by international artists. Typical of them is *L'Enterrement* ('The Burial'), by the Vannes engraver Jean Frélaut, who produced hundreds of engravings during the first half of this century. In this sombre scene a funeral procession plods across a dismal countryside beneath a lowering sky; the coffin is drawn by a windblown horse, and behind trudge the family and friends, first the men and then the women, black-clad and depressed-looking – a side of vanished peasant life ignored by the idealizing school of Breton artists. The museum part of La Cohue includes displays on the life and times of the oyster, on the *sinago* (a flat-bottomed boat found only in the Gulf of Morbihan), on the *moulins à marée* (tide-mills) which were built all round the Gulf from the Middle Ages to the nineteenth century, and on the geology, birds and beasts of this fascinating area.

Vannes Cathedral, opposite La Cohue's main entrance, is a hotchpotch of styles, ranging from the thirteenth-century romanesque of the north-west tower (Tour Romane) to the odd circular Tour Renaissance, decorated externally with pilasters and scallop shells, which was added in the sixteenth century on the north side of the nave. The tomb of St Vincent and his relics are kept here; round the walls are tapestries, woven in 1615, showing his miracles of healing. The chapel directly opposite is dedicated to the Blessed Pierre-René Rogue, a priest who was born in Vannes in 1758. During the French Revolution, when traditional

*The medieval city wall of Vannes rises above neatly tended flower-beds. In the background is the long roof of the cathedral.*

Catholic worship was proscribed by the authorities, Rogue continued to conduct services in secret, though he was hunted by the police. In 1795 he was arrested, tried and guillotined; so close was the community in those days that Rogue had known the executioner for years, and had taught him his catechism. In 1934 he was beatified by Pope Pius XI, and his remains were transferred to the cathedral.

Walk back along the ramparts from the Porte Prison, the best of the medieval gateways. This ten-minute stroll gives a good idea of the smallness of the old town, and a view of the much-photographed medieval wash-houses, which open on to what remains of the original water-filled moat. The western limit of old Vannes is marked today by the dead-straight Rue Thiers, which was carved through the ancient centre in the nineteenth century, and contains most of the municipal buildings.

Modern industrial Vannes has spread enormously, out to the *rocade* (ring road) and beyond. But there are some good buildings among the nondescript concrete, notably the smart new aquarium a kilometre south of the old town, overlooking the west side of the harbour. A startling white pyramid, with a brilliant green entrance portico looking something like the open mouth of a fish, it has the richest collection of tropical species in the whole of Europe. There is also a tank of electric eels which, when suitably annoyed, give off enough power to work a whole array of flashing light-bulbs; a crocodile 'discovered in the Paris sewers' a few years ago; and what is claimed to be the best restaurant in Vannes.

The road from Vannes round the north side of the Gulf of Morbihan (D101) begins from this general direction. You can spend a happy day pottering around such lagoonside villages as Arradon, Port-Blanc and Larmor-Baden, with endless magical vistas

*Oyster racks at low tide at Larmor-Baden, one of the lagoonside villages around the Gulf of Morbihan, Brittany's island-studded inland sea.*

*In regular use until recent times, the medieval wash-houses of Vannes are reflected in what remains of the moat that surrounded the city.*

of islands large and small, as you skirt the fringes of the inland sea. From Port-Blanc and Larmor-Baden ferries run to two of the main islands, respectively the Ile aux Moines and the Ile Gavrinis. The Ile aux Moines – so called from monks who settled there in the ninth century – is the largest island in the Gulf and is famous for the subtropical mildness of its climate; while on tiny Gavrinis is one of Morbihan's grandest neolithic passage graves, built around 3000 BC from fifty or so enormous granite slabs. Many of the stones in the passage leading to the burial chamber are carved with stylized snakes, axes and other symbolic designs, looking rather like giant fingerprints. The designs were picked out in the granite with small flakes of diamond-hard quartz, many of which have been found on the floor of the tomb.

*Neolithic carvings on the walls of a passage grave on the little island of Gavrinis, in the Gulf of Morbihan. The structure is one of the best-preserved of its kind and is about 5000 years old.*

From Larmor-Baden, drive north to Auray through Baden and Bono, stopping for the splendid estuary view from Bono's high-level bridge. Auray is a town on two levels: down by the river is the medieval port of Saint-Goustan, full of half-timbered houses and waterside cafés; and on the other side Auray proper, reached across a pretty medieval bridge either by a steep road up the hill, or by way of a zigzag tree-shaded path leading up from the waterfront.

A plaque on one of Saint-Goustan's ancient houses records the visit in 1776 of Benjamin Franklin, who landed at Auray on his way to Paris to negotiate a treaty between France and the fledgling United States. Franklin continued on to Vannes, but did not enjoy the journey, as his journal makes clear:

The carriage was a miserable one, with tired horses, the evening dark, scarce a traveller but ourselves on the road; and to make it more comfortable, the driver stopped near a wood we were to pass through, to tell us that a gang of eighteen robbers infested that wood, who but two weeks ago had robbed and murdered some travellers on that very spot.

The shopping and commercial part of Auray is up at the top of the hill, round the big seventeenth-century church. There is nothing particularly memorable about the upper town, except perhaps the streets of curious little nineteenth-century villas on the way to the station.

Auray has had a warlike past for so sleepy and peaceful a place. In 1364 the Battle of Auray, fought outside the town, put an end to the War of Succession, which decided who was to be Duke of Brittany; the victor was the Montfort Duke Jean IV, founder of the shrine at Le Folgoët. A later campaign is commemorated just north of Auray, in a field now called the Champ des Martyrs. This grassy rectangle, with a small temple at one end, was the scene of an atrocity that took place towards the end of the French Revolution. After the defeat of the Chouans (anti-Revolution royalists from Brittany and the Vendée) at Quiberon in 1795, over 200 of them were summarily tried, taken to the Champ des Martyrs, and shot.

Auray has a religious offshoot in Sainte-Anne d'Auray, 6 kilometres away along the D17. The centre of Brittany's greatest *pardon*, held at the end of July, it owes its fame to a miraculous statue of St Anne, mother of the Virgin, unearthed by a local farmer in 1623. A chapel was soon built on the site, succeeded by the present vast basilica in the 1860s. In front of it is an enormous open space for the crowds to gather, and a gigantic war memorial to the 250,000 Bretons killed in

*The Renaissance doorway of the seventeenth-century St Gildas church, Auray. In the top niche, the saint raises his hand in blessing.*

World War I. The complex is intimidatingly huge, on a scale which fortunately has been repeated nowhere else in Brittany.

The road south from Auray (D28) brings you to the part of Brittany that is richer in prehistoric remains than any similar small area in Europe. For more than 2500 years, from about 4500 BC, the great megalithic civilization of the New Stone Age covered the heath-land north of Quiberon Bay with thousands of standing stones and hundreds of chamber tombs, an achievement that must have called for powers of organization comparable to those of ancient Egypt, operating at much the same time. The standing stones are thought to have had astronomical significance, and the tombs must have been for rulers or great priests – Stone Age technology and religion working together to great effect, but for purposes that no archaeologist has yet been able to discover.

Locmariaquer, a small fishing village at the end of the D781, has several of the finest of the remains. Up a lane behind the village street, and close together, are a giant standing stone and a large chamber tomb, each among the biggest of its kind, though not the best preserved. The Grand Menhir Brisé, now lying on the ground in four broken pieces, is estimated to weigh 350 tonnes and to have stood about 20m high – almost as tall as Cleopatra's Needle, and twice as heavy. The Table des Marchand (Marchand in the singular, as it is a family name and does not mean 'merchant') is a massive chamber tomb with a capstone 6m long by 4m wide; as in many of these tombs, the stones are carved here and there with symbolic designs. Until recently you could wander freely round them; but they are now fenced in, and you have to pay to see them. A Stone Age graveyard on the site is at present (1990) being excavated.

A brilliant piece of archaeological detective work links the Table des Marchand with the passage grave on Gavrinis. Among the carvings on the capstone over the Gavrinis burial chamber are the sweeping horns of an ox-like animal, without a head or body to go with them. During the 1980s a sharp-eyed archaeologist spotted the rest of the beast on the Table des Marchand capstone, and found that it fitted perfectly with the Gavrinis carving. A third large slab from elsewhere in Locmariaquer matched the other end of the Gavrinis stone – proof that all three slabs originally came from a giant menhir, 14m high. The Grand Menhir Brisé is no doubt another example of such Stone Age recycling, divided into four potential capstones but never removed. Historians of prehistory think that the menhirs may have been broken up by a later, dolmen-building civilization, in much the same way that Christians broke up the stones of Roman temples and built them into their churches.

Just south of Locmariaquer, beside the beach, is another well-preserved chamber tomb. Called the Dolmen des Pierres Plates (though its stones are not noticeably flat), it is a long passage grave with a kink in the middle and a little side passage like a chapel. If you shuffle along it holding a torch, you can just about make out the carvings on the walls, among them a human torso with fernlike ribs, and a multi-breasted female figure, perhaps the guardian goddess of the ruler for whom the tomb was built.

The Locmariaquer peninsula tapers away to the Pointe de Kerpenhir, an undramatic headland beside the narrow, fast-flowing channel that leads into the Gulf of Morbihan. A German blockhouse, still containing chunks of rusty metal that were once a gun, squats on the headland looking across the channel towards the Rhuys peninsula, while below on the rocks a statue of the Virgin gives protection to the yachts dancing in and out of the gulf.

Leaving Locmariaquer, follow the D781 round to the yachting and oyster centre of La Trinité-sur-Mer and on to Carnac. Carnac is renowned throughout the archaeological world for its *alignements* – those ten or more striding lines of menhirs, stretching into the distance across the gorse-covered heathland like a fossilized army on parade. Along with Stonehenge and

---

*A medieval bridge leads across the Auray river to the medieval quayside of Saint-Goustan, below the town of Auray.*

Avebury in England, the standing stones of Carnac rank as the largest and most impressive constructions of Stone Age man. Early writers peopled them with Druids carrying out ghastly rituals of human sacrifice; while in Breton legend they are said to have been brought to Carnac on the backs of a race of brawny and hairy elves known as the Korred. As mentioned above, today's archaeologists and scholars cannot agree on their significance, though it seems probable that they were set up by a caste of priest-kings as giant observatories linked to the movement of the heavenly bodies. With exclusive knowledge of the correct dates for sowing and harvesting, such experts would be in a position of commanding authority among a primitive farming population.

In the *alignements*, and in the surrounding country-side, there are about 5000 menhirs altogether. The three main *alignements* run roughly from south-west to north-east: Ménec, about a kilometre long by 100m wide; Kermario (the name in Breton means 'House of the Dead'), covering much the same extent; and Kerlescan, slightly shorter and correspondingly wider. The road runs right alongside them, and in summer there are so many crawling cars that it is much better to walk. During high season the *alignements* swarm with people, walking among the stones and even climbing up them. As a result, some of the menhirs are suffering severely from the onslaught; and it cannot be long before they are fenced off, as at Stonehenge, though at Carnac the problems of fencing and patrolling such a vast area would be far greater.

For years Carnac's excellent museum of prehistory, the Musée Miln-Le Rouzic, was a cramped, old-fashioned kind of place; but it has recently been moved to more spacious quarters beside the village square, and is now as up-to-date a museum as you will find anywhere. It was founded by James Miln, a Scottish amateur archaeologist who began work at

*Some of the thousands of menhirs or standing stones that make up the neolithic alignements of Carnac.*

Carnac in 1874; his chief assistant, Zacharie Le Rouzic, took over the excavations and the collection that forms the nucleus of the museum when Miln died suddenly in 1881. Le Rouzic's work at Carnac continued until his death in 1939; his sixty years of research at the same site must surely be an archaeological record.

The museum is full of objects from a high civilization, meticulously laid out and placed in their context – jadeite polished axes, decorated pottery, gold ornaments, bead necklaces, tools such as drills and scrapers. Graphic panels show how menhirs were raised and dolmens constructed. Erecting a menhir was comparatively simple: the stone was brought to the site on rollers, lowered into a hole and hauled upright until it rested against a wooden backing prop; the hole was filled and packed solid round the base of the stone, and the prop was removed. The building of a dolmen began with setting the uprights in the same way. When the walls of the corridor and burial chamber were in position, the space between them was filled with earth, and earth ramps were constructed outside. The roof stones were hauled up the ramp on rollers until they overlapped the walls; the corridor and chamber were cleared of earth; and the completed tomb was covered with a turfed-over mound.

Such a mound still exists virtually unaltered a few hundred metres from the centre of Carnac. The Tumulus Saint-Michel is a huge construction, 125m long by 60m wide, made of two layers of stone with an earth layer between. The lower layer contained burial chambers, whose contents are now in the museum. On top of the mound is a small chapel dedicated to St Michael, and from the platform on which it stands there are wide views over the whole megalith area and far out to sea. In earlier centuries the locals believed that Julius Caesar was buried under the mound in a golden coffin, no doubt a distorted folk-memory of the treasure-crammed tombs of neolithic kings, combined with the giant shadow cast across the centuries by Brittany's Roman conqueror.

Archaeology apart, Carnac is well worth visiting in its own right, as it is a pretty little town, with some of Morbihan's finest beaches at Carnac Plage just down the road. Experts tell us that Carnac's name has nothing to do with the Egyptian Karnak, though the typical tumulus beside Quiberon Bay, with its central chamber and mound above, bears a strong family resemblance to the typical pyramid beside the Nile. It derives either from the Breton *karn*, meaning 'horn', or is the same as the Gaelic word *cairn*, meaning a heap of stones on a burial mound. Probably the former is correct, since the patron saint of Carnac is St Cornély, or Cornelius, who is also the patron saint of all horned animals. The big renaissance church, with a tower built in 1639, is dedicated to him, and his statue stands on its outside wall between two oxen.

Cornelius is said to have been one of the early popes, martyred in 252 or 253 under the Emperor Decius, and he is always portrayed with the papal tiara on his head. The explanation of how he got to Brittany is even more far-fetched than most of such legends. Pursued from Rome by hostile pagans, he headed north and then west through Italy and Gaul, on a chariot drawn by two oxen. When he reached Carnac, he turned and saw the pagan army marching towards him in regular columns, whereupon he uttered a curse which turned the troops to stone; they have been standing there, rank on rank, ever since.

The link between Cornelius and horned animals is maintained by the annual blessing of the cattle held in his honour on September 13, which is near the autumn equinox, and may date back as far as pre-Christian times. James Miln, founder of the Carnac museum, described a strange ritual that must surely be pagan. When sick cattle had to be cured, they were driven in solemn silence from the farm to Carnac church, and from there to the fountain of Saint-Cornély, where water was poured over them. Then in the same silence the journey was reversed, and they were driven back past the church and so home. Cattle were also made to

*Waves rolling in from the Atlantic break along the sea-front at Quiberon, one of Brittany's fastest-growing resorts.*

pass through the smoke of the bonfires lit on Midsummer Eve (June 24), which was believed to keep them from disease the following year. As a primitive form of fumigation, it was no doubt reasonably effective.

Leaving Carnac, drive west to Plouharnel, and then turn down the Quiberon Peninsula. This long finger of land, pointing due south for 15 kilometres, is really an island joined to the mainland by a sandy isthmus. It protects the waters of Quiberon Bay from the pounding force of the Atlantic rollers, and thus has two very different aspects: on the east side a sheltered sandy coast lined with holiday homes, and on the west the rocky and dramatic Côte Sauvage, as dangerous as any stretch of the Breton coast. The twisting road along the Côte Sauvage leaves the D768 about half-way down the peninsula, and runs past expanses of springy turf leading down to the rocks. Though the sandy creeks look inviting enough, signs in French, English and German warn would-be swimmers that 'this coast is very dangerous even if the sea seems to be calm'. Above one such creek is an obelisk commemorating a gendarme and a fireman, who in 1979 gave their lives in an attempt to save *un imprudent* from drowning.

Quiberon town, at the end of the peninsula, is a cheerfully brash resort, which is expanding round the coast and inland up the main road. The local hero is General Hoche (1768–97), whose statue stands beside the public gardens just off the sea-front. Hoche was one of the ablest of the young commanders produced by the Revolution; in 1794, aged only 26, he was appointed to command the Revolutionary forces fighting the royalist Chouans in Brittany and the Vendée. At the end of a successful campaign he forced about 20,000 Chouans, including women and children, down to the end of the peninsula. Many of them managed to escape by sea, but several hundred were captured, among them the 200 who, as described above, were shot in the Champ des Martyrs outside Auray, much against the wishes of Hoche himself.

Quiberon's harbour is the starting-point for the ferry to Belle-Ile, Brittany's largest offshore island; the crossing to Le Palais, its little capital, takes about three-quarters of an hour. Its 80 kilometres of coastline, contrasting rocky headlands with small beaches and creeks, makes it a favourite with both holidaymakers and artists. Monet, Derain and Matisse came here to paint, while among writers Dumas, Flaubert and Proust visited the island. Unlike the smaller Breton islands such as Ouessant, where you are always conscious of the sea close at hand, Belle-Ile has enough woods, valleys and inland villages to create the illusion that it is part of the mainland. The best way to see it in a day is to get an early boat from Quiberon and hire a bicycle at Le Palais.

Apart from Le Palais, there are only three other places of any size: Bangor, which shares its name with the Welsh city, Locmaria, and Sauzon, whose name is Breton for 'Saxon' or 'English'. The English connection became a reality in 1761, during the Seven Years War, when British troops conquered Belle-Ile and occupied it for two years, exchanging it in 1763 for Canada under the Treaty of Paris. During this short period the English succeeded in introducing the potato to the island, but otherwise their influence was minimal.

The ferry slides into Le Palais harbour through an entrance so narrow that you wonder how the helmsman avoids hitting the jetty. Above the harbour loom the great stone walls of the Citadelle, one of Brittany's most formidable fortresses, which alone would make a visit to Belle-Ile well worth while. The rocky spur on which it stands was occupied from the earliest times; in the eleventh century monks from Redon built a monastery on the site; but it was not properly fortified until the mid sixteenth century. Throughout the seventeenth century the defences were gradually strengthened, reaching their present size and scale in the 1680s under Vauban. After the British occupation of 1761–3, the citadel became a barracks, then a prison (last used during the 1950s for Algerian freedom fighters), and since 1960 has been privately owned.

---

*Twin lighthouses guard the narrow entrance to the harbour of Le Palais on Belle-Ile, Brittany's largest offshore island.*

The way in takes you between vast walls pierced with cannon embrasures and through the Porte du Donjon, a noble classical gateway crowned by a pediment carved with fasces and trophies of war. Once inside, you are surrounded by a bewildering complex of buildings of every period: sinister dungeons from the sixteenth-century fortress, with notices reading *Ne craignez rien – entrez* ('Fear not – enter'); a huge eighteenth-century barrack block still with its latrines and prison cells; bastions laid out with paths and flower-beds; and a comfortable house that looks like a Breton *manoir*, where the present proprietor lives. Most unusual of all is the circular powder-magazine, built around 1650 and said to be on the site of the monks' chapel. Inside, its walls and domed roof have an acoustic effect which makes even the smallest sound fully audible. The panorama from the ramparts takes in Quiberon, the lesser islands of Houat and Hoëdic, and the mainland beyond, and makes it clear why Belle-Ile has been of such strategic value down the centuries.

One of the buildings by the entrance has been turned into a fascinating museum, where you can browse among exquisitely drawn plans of redoubts and casemates, or look at nineteenth-century photographs of boat-building and tuna-fishing. A whole section is devoted to the actress Sarah Bernhardt, who in 1886 bought and restored an old fortress at the Pointe des Poulains, the northern tip of the island, and turned it into a summer retreat. There are playbills advertising some of her most famous roles (Froufrou, Mélisande, La Dame aux Camélias) and photographs showing her in them, dresses and parasols, and a set of ten postcards that fit together to form a composite portrait. Though on the evidence of the photographs she was no beauty, she must have had an electric stage personality – at least, if one can trust the portrait *Mme Sarah Bernhardt in a Rage*, which shows her with glaring eyes and hair starting up like a porcupine's quills.

*A waterside shrine below the chapel of Saint-Cado, a fishing village on an island in the Rivière d'Etel. The shrine may have been used for baptisms.*

What the stolid Bellilois peasants made of her is not recorded; but they must have shaken their heads over her household menagerie with its wildcat and boa-constrictor, and her habit of going out at six in the morning to shoot duck or seagulls, accompanied by a small black boy and two enormous mastiffs.

Head back up the Quiberon peninsula to Plouharnel, and turn north-west along the D781. On either side of the dead-straight road the heathland is strewn with holiday homes, dolmens and menhirs – a curious and incongruous mixture of the twentieth centuries AD and BC. Beyond Erdeven, the coast is cut deeply by the Rivière de l'Etel, not so much a river as an inland lagoon dotted with islands, like a small relation of the Gulf of Morbihan. On one of the islands, now linked to the mainland by a causeway, is the pretty fishing village of Saint-Cado, well worth hunting out along the back roads. The chapel, built in the twelfth century but much altered since, faces a row of fishermen's cottages across a wide green. Beside it is a large calvary and open-air pulpit, approached by a triple flight of stairs; and behind it is a tiny stone shrine right on the edge of the water, with a surrounding wall, cruciform in plan, that looks as though it was built for baptism by total immersion.

According to a doggerel rhyme painted round the inside wall of the chapel, Cado was a Welsh prince who was born in Glamorgan, served as a priest in Brittany, and was finally driven out by pirates. Legend has it that he contrived to outwit the Devil, who had agreed to build a bridge from the island to the mainland, provided he could have the soul of the first creature to cross it. With the help of his mother, the Devil built the bridge in a single night and sat back waiting for Cado to walk over it; but the wily saint sent a cat across it, and the Prince of Darkness was foiled once again.

Continue across the Etel to Port-Louis, once a naval port as important as Brest, but sunk for three centuries or so in somnolent obscurity. Port-Louis stands on a spit of land guarding the wide combined estuary of the Scorff and Blavet rivers; its huge and impressive Citadelle is comparable to that of Belle-Ile. Originally a fishing village called Blavet, it was renamed in honour of Louis XIII early in the seventeenth century. The citadel was begun in 1590 and completed under Cardinal Richelieu in 1637; its great stone bastions, projecting like the points of a star into the estuary, are a textbook example of early seventeenth-century fortification.

Soon after the citadel was built, the Compagnie des Indes – the French equivalent of Britain's East India Company – set up its headquarters at Port-Louis, but towards the end of the century it moved across the estuary to Lorient, and Port-Louis fell into decline. It is now a quiet but hauntingly memorable little town, with ramparts and curtain wall that seem far too large and impressive for so small a place. From its tree-shaded walks you can look across the estuary, crowded with cargo-boats, naval corvettes, ferries, yachts and even the occasional rowing skiff, to the modern tower blocks of Lorient on the other side of the water.

The citadel has been turned into a splendid museum – or rather, museums, as there are several different collections within its walls. The main collection, the Musée de la Compagnie des Indes, is housed in a sprawling block with no fewer than fifteen inter-connected rooms, and is crammed with the oriental treasures accumulated by trade and by conquest. The Compagnie lasted from 1664 until the Revolution, and for well over a century France ran neck and neck with Britain in colonizing and plundering the known world. West Africa, Madagascar, Mauritius, India, Thailand, China: each of them has its own section, illustrated with maps and drawings, cases of exotic clothes, armour and porcelain, and displays on saffron, pepper, tea and coffee.

Among the fascinating exhibits is a cut-away model of the pride of the Compagnie's eighteenth-century fleet, the 1200-tonne *Comte d'Artois*, complete with 300 tiny figures of blue-coated officers, periwigged passengers and pigtailed crew. Virtually the entire vessel below the waterline was taken up with cargo – though, this being a French ship, there was also a large *caveau du capitaine* for the commanding officer's food and wine.

To get from Port-Louis to Lorient, you can either drive upstream to the bridge across the Blavet and then down again to the town centre; or take the ferry that chugs across the estuary every hour or so. This half-hour trip is well worth making, as it gives constantly changing views of the estuary, and lands you right in the old harbour of Lorient. The half-way point finds you equidistant between two very different fortifications built three centuries apart – the graceful ravelins of the Port-Louis Citadelle, and the hulking concrete submarine pens built at Lorient by the Germans during World War II, which are still used by the French navy, and look as though nothing short of an atom bomb would dislodge them.

As mentioned above, Lorient (originally L'Orient) succeeded Port-Louis as the headquarters of the Compagnie des Indes. In 1770 the French navy took over the harbour, and Lorient has remained an important naval base ever since. At the end of World War II it was fiercely defended by the Germans, and was virtually destroyed by the Allies; as a result, it has been almost entirely rebuilt in a faceless modern style, though there are still a few old buildings from the time of the Compagnie des Indes in the streets leading off the harbour. As at Brest, only French nationals are allowed to visit the naval installations.

Though architecturally Lorient may not be much to look at, for the past twenty years it has been one of the centres of the Breton cultural revival. Each August its ten-day Festival Interceltique brings together more than 4000 musicians, dancers, actors and artists of every description, not just from Brittany, but from Scotland, Ireland, Wales, the Isle of Man and Cornwall, and from Galicia and Asturias in northern Spain. If you visit Lorient during the festival, on every street corner you will hear the squeals and groans of bagpipes being tuned, and see girls from Galicia or Guingamp patting

*Like the prow of a stone battleship, a bastion of the seventeenth-century citadel of Port-Louis juts into the Scorff estuary. The citadel is now the museum of the Compagnie des Indes.*

their lace head-dresses into shape, before joining one of the processions that block the main streets for hours at a time. The football stadium, ten minutes' walk from the harbour, is crammed with dancers in traditional costume, the tree-lined green that stretches down to the harbour is turned into a fairground, and schools, churches and halls of every kind are given over to concerts and fringe events. At Lorient even the hamburgers have a Celtic flavour: rechristened Breiz-burgers (from Breiz, the Breton for Brittany), they are made of guaranteed Breton meat.

The ferry over to the Ile de Groix leaves from Lorient's quayside. The boat trip takes about 45 minutes, and is an even better way of seeing the Blavet estuary than the ferry between Lorient and Port-Louis. In many ways Groix is a small sister of Belle-Ile, and is linked with it, and with Ouessant, third of the major island trio, in an ancient jingle:

*Qui voit Belle-Ile, voit son île.*
*Qui voit Groix, voit sa joie.*
*Qui voit Ouessant, voit son sang.*


('Whoever sees Belle-Ile, sees his own island.
Whoever sees Groix, sees his happiness.
Whoever sees Ushant, sees his own blood.')

Like Belle-Ile, Groix has a mild climate and a sleepy feeling about it, quite unlike the rugged, windswept uplands of Ouessant. Its Breton name, Enez ar Groac'h, means 'Island of the Witch', though nowadays there are no obvious covens to be seen. If you hire a bicycle at the neat little harbour of Port-Tudy, you can easily see Groix in a day. In spite of its small size – it is only about 7 kilometres long – it has plenty of contrast, from the bird sanctuary by the Pen-Men lighthouse at its western end, to the extraordinary mica-filled rocks at the Pointe du Chat, its eastern extremity, which glitter

---

*The fifteenth-century wall and turreted Broërec Gate of Hennebont, an old town that was badly damaged in World War II.*

with millions of tiny crystals when the sun strikes them. Port-Tudy has a small local museum, with displays on the island's long-vanished fishing industry, and a retired lifeboat whose dozens of rescues down the years are proudly recorded round the walls.

Returning from Lorient to Port-Louis on the ferry, head north to the ancient town of Hennebont. Its name comes from the Breton Hen Bont, meaning 'Old Bridge', as it stands at the first point at which the Blavet estuary could be bridged by medieval building methods. Like Lorient, it was greatly damaged during World War II and is thus largely new; but a good stretch of the medieval castle wall survives down by the river. During the fourteenth-century War of Succession between the Bretons and the French, the castle was defended by Jeanne of Flanders, the wife of Jean de Montfort, against the French army. One night she sallied out from the castle and set fire to the French camp, winning the nickname 'Jeanne la Flamme', and a lasting reputation as a Breton patriot. Hennebont's sixteenth-century church, up the hill from the castle, has an eye-catching tower and spire 65m high, and an enormously tall western porch.

Drive east towards Baud along the N24 and take the 'Centre Ville' road. A kilometre before the town a signpost directs you to the 'Vénus de Quinipily'. One of Morbihan's unexplained enigmas, her statue stands on a hillside between a farm and an orchard, perched on top of a stone canopy behind a huge stone tank. She is quite unlike the beautiful goddess you might expect from her name: squat-bodied and thin-limbed, she is naked except for a head-band and a scarf that falls below her waist. She looks Egyptian, even Red Indian, and has been identified variously as Cybele, as Isis, the Egyptian goddess worshipped by the Roman legionaries, as an unknown goddess of the Gauls, or as a fake.

Until the seventeenth century she stood on a hill 12 kilometres north of Baud, on the site of a Gaulish settlement. She was known as *Ar Gwreg Houarn* ('The Iron Woman'), and was venerated by the local peasants to such a degree that the Bishop of Vannes had her torn down and thrown into the Blavet. In 1696 the Seigneur de Quinipily retrieved her and set her up where she

*The Château de Josselin's domestic range, built by Jean de Rohan about 1500. The narrow gothic-looking gables are embellished with extravagant renaissance decoration.*

turned into an imaginative open-air gallery of modern sculpture, run by the Ministry of Culture in collaboration with the Morbihan *département*, who own Kerguéhennec. The sculptures are widely spaced among the trees, on the lawns, and by the artificial lake below the château, so that, walking round the park, you suddenly catch sight of a cluster of tall bronze pillars at the end of a grassy alley, or are brought up short by a monster construction that looks like a cross between a dinosaur and a combine harvester. Inside the magnificent nineteenth-century greenhouse is an array of a thousand red-painted concrete flowerpots, arranged in rows on the floor and along the shelves like the potting-shed of some gigantic gardener. Whether the sculptures have any great merit as works of art time alone will tell; but it is surely most unusual, and encouraging, to find a local authority not only saving a fine château and its parkland, but providing a setting in which controversial works by modern artists can be seen to their greatest advantage.

Back on the main road (N24), head for Josselin, 15 kilometres to the east. The little town huddles for protection round the mighty feudal castle of the Rohans, one of Brittany's most powerful families during the Middle Ages and later. The castle's three majestic towers, sheer-walled and conical-roofed, rise from the rock above the calm waters of the River Oust, and must be the most photographed architectural panorama in Brittany. Until about 1000 AD the town was known as Thro, but during the eleventh century a Breton lord called Josselin became its *seigneur* and gave it his own name. The castle he built was attacked by the English in the 1160s and largely destroyed. Towards the end of the fourteenth century it was rebuilt on a far grander scale by Olivier de Clisson; rising straight from the river bank, as it did then, it must have seemed impregnable.

now stands, gazing across a fertile little valley, and guarding the mystery of her origins.

Head next for Locminé, 16 kilometres east of Baud. This small market town, on the little Tarun river, grew up round an abbey founded in the seventh century; its name means 'City of the Monks' in Breton. The seventeenth-century church has an extraordinary modern annexe on the north side, looking like a vast lean-to, constructed of wood and slate, and lit by huge windows.

From Locminé, drive 5 kilometres east to the village of Bignan, and from there take a back road to Kerguéhennec, an eighteenth-century château lost in the depths of the countryside. With its symmetrical façade and formal gardens flanked by long pavilions, the château would be worth visiting in its own right; but what makes it exceptional is that its park has been

*The towers of the Château de Josselin rise proudly from the banks of the Oust. One of Brittany's finest castles, it combines a warlike medieval exterior with a spectacular renaissance inner courtyard.*

Clisson's exploits during the Hundred Years War gained him the title 'Butcher of the English'. In 1380 he was appointed Constable of France, in command of all the armed forces of the realm, and his motto, *Pour ce qui me plest* ('I do as I please'), reveals the extent of his arrogance and power. Clisson was outdone in self-display by his successors, the Rohans, who married into his family and own Josselin to this day. About 1500, Jean de Rohan built the spectacular internal domestic quarters (*corps-de-logis*), an early renaissance (or late gothic) showpiece of narrow gables, fretted pinnacles and decorative stonework balustrades, which makes a delightfully frivolous contrast to the grim military appearance of the outer walls. If you look closely at the carving, you can see in several places the Rohan motto *A plus* ('Even more', or 'To excess'), together with the initial 'A' of the Duchess Anne, and the crown of the King of France, to whom she was married. More often than not the letters are carved in the shape of writhing sea-monsters. The device of initials and *A plus* motto was carried over into the interior, notably above the fireplace in the Grand Salon, one of the ground-floor rooms open to the public, where they are picked out in gold on a red background. After the Revolution the château fell into disrepair, until major restoration in the nineteenth century brought it back to life again.

A block of outbuildings has been turned into a doll museum, to display the collection of the Rohan family down the years. Entered from the street, not from the castle, it has hundreds of examples from France and elsewhere in Europe, some dating back to the eighteenth century, along with exotic Japanese, Russian and even Hopi Indian dolls. It is the perfect museum for a wet Brittany afternoon, especially for anyone with young children. As an unexpected bonus, its windows give a clear view across the château's inner courtyard to the *corps-de-logis* beyond.

*The timbers of this sixteenth-century house in Ploërmel are carved with caryatid-like figures that seem to support the weight of the building.*

*Malestroit has several amusing painted carvings on the timbers of its medieval houses, among them this bagpipe-playing hare.*

Apart from the castle, there is plenty to see in the town centre, with its half-timbered houses that jut across the narrow streets, and its superb gothic church, founded in the eleventh century and dedicated to Notre Dame du Roncier ('Our Lady of the Bramble-thicket'), whose cult goes back to the time long before Josselin had its present name. Some time in the ninth century, a peasant from Thro, walking beside the Oust, found a miraculous bramble bush that kept its leaves even in the depths of winter, and in the centre of the bush an archaic wooden statue of the Virgin. He took the statue home, but by the next morning he found that it was back in the thicket. After this had happened several times, the local clergy took note, and a chapel was built for the statue on the site of the bush. It was eventually moved to the town's main church, but it was burnt in 1789 as an object of

159

superstition. The statue that now stands in the church is a replica made in 1868. The *pardon* of Notre Dame du Roncier is held early in September; it was formerly known also as the Pardon des Aboyeuses ('Pardon of the Barking Women'), from the epileptics who attended it in the hope of a miraculous cure.

Drive next to Ploërmel, 12 kilometres east of Josselin. At the half-way point the dual carriageway N24 splits in two, leaving an elongated traffic island, with one of Brittany's most historic monuments standing on it among the trees. Known as the Colonne des Trente ('Column of the Thirties', in the plural), it celebrates a famous feat of arms that took place in 1351, during the War of Succession. The garrison at Josselin was commanded by a Breton, Jean de Beaumanoir, while English mercenaries under Robert Bemborough held Ploërmel for the French. The commanders agreed to battle it out at an oak-tree half way between the two towns (the Chêne de Mi-Voie), with thirty knights on each side. The two sides fought all day, until the English knights were routed; the survivors were taken back to Josselin and ransomed. In the course of the battle Beaumanoir was wounded and lost a lot of blood. When he called out for a drink, one of his men answered '*Bois ton sang, Beaumanoir, ta soif se passera*' ('Drink your blood, Beaumanoir, your thirst will pass') – a reply that has become proverbial.

Ploërmel is a busy crossroads town, badly damaged towards the end of World War II. It gets its name from St Armel, a sixth-century British monk, who won a reputation for sanctity by taming a dragon and leading it around on the end of his stole (St Pol did the same thing on the Ile de Batz, by Roscoff). The magnificent church is mainly sixteenth-century Flamboyant gothic; the spire was destroyed by a shell during the war and has not been rebuilt. There is a very fine stained-glass window with a Tree of Jesse, and some earlier fifteenth-century glass illustrating the life of St

*A jumble of ancient façades in the small flower-filled town of Rochefort-en-Terre, which stands on a hill above a river valley.*

*Hazelnuts for sale in the market at Rochefort-en-Terre.*

Armel. Ploërmel's chief curiosity is an astronomical clock, in a courtyard near the church. Built by a monk in the 1850s, it is a superb piece of craftsmanship, with ten dials giving the time both local and world-wide, the positions of the moon, earth and sun, and a view of the heavens as seen from Ploërmel.

Drive south along the N166, then take the D764 for Malestroit. One of the most delightful old towns of Morbihan, Malestroit is beautifully sited by the Oust, which here forms part of the Nantes-Brest Canal, and is the perfect place for a waterside stroll. Its name derives from its poor communications in medieval times, *mala strata* (Latin for 'bad road') becoming Malestroit. There are plenty of medieval houses, many of them slate-hung, in and around the main square; the timber-framed Maison de La Truie qui File ('House of the Spinning Sow') gets its name from the humorous painted statue on one of its beam-ends. The church, dedicated to St Gilles, is basically twelfth-century romanesque, greatly enlarged in the sixteenth century by the addition of a second nave. The side doorway into the church is exceptionally fine; on either side are animal statues, a lion for St Mark and an ox for St Luke. At some point in the afternoon the shadow cast by the ox on the wall of the church is said to resemble the profile of the arch-sceptic Voltaire.

During World War II the wild wooded country south and west of Malestroit, known as the Landes de Lanvaux, was one of the centres of the Breton Resistance movement. At the time of the Allied invasion of France in June 1944, the Landes saw a heroic operation against the Germans by a combined force of French paratroopers and members of the Resistance. A full-scale pitched battle took place near the village of Saint-Marcel, just west of Malestroit, commemorated by a tall memorial column.

In Saint-Marcel's Musée de la Résistance Bretonne you can trace the whole history of the Resistance movement in Brittany, from its spontaneous beginnings, through the setting-up of a countrywide network of cells, to the Battle of Saint-Marcel and the liberation of Brittany two months later. For those not in the Resistance life went on as normal, given the circumstances: an especially telling photograph, taken in 1941, shows a girl on Malestroit bridge having her papers inspected by a German soldier. The bridge is still as it was half a century ago, but the Germans now come to Malestroit as peaceful tourists. Scattered under the trees round about are World War II tanks, lorries, guns and other assorted hardware of that far-off conflict.

Drive 17 kilometres south to Rochefort-en-Terre, a jewel of an old town, which stands on a hilly site above the Gueuzon valley, with steps leading from one level to another. Many towns in Brittany claim to be *villes fleuries*, but Rochefort outdoes all its rivals in the number of its geranium-filled window-boxes and stone troughs. The large church, a short way down the hill from the main street, is mainly sixteenth-century Flamboyant gothic, with a twelfth-century romanesque tower, and an ancient calvary beside it. It is dedicated to Notre Dame de la Tronchaye, a *tronchaie*

being a cluster of tree-trunks, where a miraculous statue of the Virgin was discovered by a shepherdess in the twelfth century, after being hidden 300 years earlier at the time of the Norman invasions. Inside the church there are some painted statues, a renaissance altar-piece, and choir stalls with fine misericords, a rarity in Brittany.

At the top of the town is a commanding plateau surrounded by the massive walls of the medieval castle, of which little else is left apart from the fortified gateway. Built in the eleventh or twelfth century, probably on the site of a Roman fort, it was extended and strengthened throughout the Middle Ages, damaged during the dynastic struggles for the Duchy of Brittany and the sixteenth-century religious wars, and finally demolished during the Revolution. Only the stables survived more or less intact, to become the nucleus of today's château.

It owes its existence to an American artist, Alfred Klots, who came to Rochefort in 1903, fell in love with the castle, bought it, and set about transforming the former stables into the present dainty renaissance-style mansion, taking much of his building materials from decaying properties in the neighbourhood. Alfred was succeeded at Rochefort by his son Trafford Klots, also a painter, who lived there until his death in 1976. During World War II Trafford Klots was an officer in the American army, and at the Liberation in 1944 he was the first man to enter Rochefort, at the head of his victorious troops. The Klots father-and-son tradition is preserved intact today. The rooms are full of the furniture and *objets-d'art* collected by them over their 70-year occupancy; and the walls are hung with their paintings, mainly portraits by Alfred and landscape drawings by Trafford. The château now belongs to the Département de Morbihan.

A little way south-east of Rochefort, near the village of Malansac, a disused slate quarry has been turned into a Parc de Préhistoire, where you can follow an outdoor trail for an hour or so past life-size mock-ups of scenes from the Stone Age. Hunters stand poised on a rock ready to hurl their spears at a reindeer on the other side of a ravine; the men and women of a Cro-

Magnon village sit outside their wigwams making a fire, stitching skins and smoking fish; straining neolithic tribesmen haul a menhir into position. Apart from being a worthwhile attempt to inject reality into Morbihan's prehistory, the park makes imaginative use of the quarry workings, creating an attractive landscape from vast holes in the ground which are now small lakes, and spoil tips which have been thickly planted with trees.

Head next for the market town of Redon, 26 kilometres to the east. Redon is Brittany's main chestnut-growing centre and is famous for its *marrons glacés*; but the main reason for going there is to see its magnificent basilica of Saint-Sauveur, once the church of the Benedictine monastery founded here in the ninth century. Above the central crossing rises one of the architectural glories of southern Brittany – the arcaded romanesque tower, built in the twelfth century, with dumpy round arches open to the winds. Its unique shape is matched by its stone, which consists of grey granite and dark red sandstone, used at random to give the appearance of a building hewn from the natural rock. In complete contrast is the tall gothic bell-tower, which has been isolated from the main church since a fire in 1780 destroyed most of the nave.

Drive west from Redon along the D20, through Muzillac to the Rhuys Peninsula, which forms a protecting arm along the southern side of the Gulf of Morbihan. Sarzeau, the only town of any size on the peninsula, has some good seventeenth-century houses with carved window-frames. The church has some curious capitals, several of them decorated with bird motifs, and two good statues of saints – Isidore, dressed as a Breton peasant in breeches, and Cornelius, the patron saint of farm animals. Most people bypass Sarzeau and press on to Port-Navalo, the main yachting and touring centre, and the starting-point for boat trips all round the gulf. From Port-Navalo you look across the narrow strait to the Pointe de Kerpenhir – only a few hundred metres over the water, but 60 kilometres or more by road, as there is no bridge.

Just along the coast is the vast new marina of Crouesty, where moorings crammed with all the latest

*This arcaded twelfth-century romanesque bell tower rises above the central crossing of the Saint-Sauveur basilica, Redon. It is built in a mixture of granite and sandstone.*

examples of yachting technology stretch along a narrow creek. Behind the jetties is a small town of off-the-peg houses for the boat-mad, where, as an unenthusiastic bystander told me, 'you can order a Norman or Breton façade like a dish at a restaurant'. In the old days, sailors passing the chapel on Crouesty's headland would take off their hats and lower their flags three times in honour of the Virgin.

By the main road east of Crouesty is a burial-mound known as the Butte de César, which gives splendid views of the yachts skimming about in Quiberon Bay. It gets its name from the story – which is probably true – that during his conquest of Gaul Julius Caesar stood here to watch his fleet destroy the navy of the Veneti. The Gauls were in high-sided ships built of oak, with

leather sails, designed for sailing the open waters well offshore, while Caesar's fleet consisted of galleys propelled by oars. When the wind dropped, the Veneti were left becalmed, and all the Romans had to do to incapacitate them was to hook their rigging with long poles and snap the ropes by rowing hard away. The Veneti surrendered, and Caesar put the seal on his victory by executing their leaders and selling the population into slavery.

A side road leads down to Saint-Gildas de Rhuys, now a holiday village, but in the Middle Ages out in the wilds of Brittany. A Welsh monk, Gildas or Gweltas, founded a monastery here in the sixth century; before coming to Brittany, he is credited with having converted Taliesin, the greatest of the Welsh bards, to Christianity. The present seventeenth-century church still has its romanesque choir and apse, with the saint's tomb behind the high altar. St Gildas's chief claim to fame comes from its connection with Peter Abelard, the great twelfth-century teacher and philosopher, whose relationship with Héloïse is one of the classic love stories of all time. Born near Nantes in 1079, Abelard became a teacher, setting up a school in Paris, where one of his pupils was Héloïse, twenty years his junior. She became his mistress and bore him a son who was given the curious name Astrolabe, rather as though a scientifically minded couple today were to call their child Space Shuttle or Electron Microscope; whereupon her uncle, a canon of Notre Dame, had him brutally castrated, and Héloïse entered a convent.

After courting theological controversy with some of his writings and teachings, and being accused of heresy, Abelard took refuge from the world at St Gildas, where he was appointed abbot in 1126. He hated the place, finding the local population 'brutal and barbarous', and the monks 'beyond control and leading a dissolute life'. According to his auto-biography – called, with some justice, *Historia Calamitatum* (*The Story of My Misfortunes*) – they tried to poison him on several occasions, and bribed robbers to murder him outside the monastery walls. After putting up with St Gildas for some years, Abelard returned to Paris to teach. He died at Cluny monastery in Burgundy in 1142, leaving as his literary testament his autobiography, philosophical works, a series of passionate letters to Héloïse, and a handful of Latin hymns.

Before leaving the Rhuys Peninsula and heading back to Vannes, drive to the Château de Suscinio, just inland from the coast. The most uncompromisingly pugnacious of all Brittany's castles, it stands so near the shore that when it was built its moat filled and emptied with the tides. The name is said to derive from the old French *souci n'y ot*, meaning 'without care' – something of a misnomer, as Suscinio has had its fair share of troubles. It was built between the thirteenth and the sixteenth centuries, which accounts for the contrast between the stark grandeur of the external walls and the luxury of the accommodation within: each bedroom, for example, has its own window seat, fireplace and lavatory annexe. The castle is being gradually restored as far as possible to its original form.

The fourteenth-century War of Succession left its mark on Suscinio, in the form of a stretch of wall built in grey stone, in contrast to the mottled brown and yellow on either side. Known as 'Du Guesclin's Breach', it was made in 1373 by Du Guesclin during his recapture of the castle from the English. During the Revolution Suscinio was used as a stone quarry, and was held for a time by the Chouans during the Quiberon campaign of 1795. Its military solidity has a tenuous link with the legendary world, for the fairy Mélusine is said to haunt its underground tunnels.

*The entrance bridge and towers of the Château of Suscinio, which stands near the sea on the Rhuys Peninsula.*

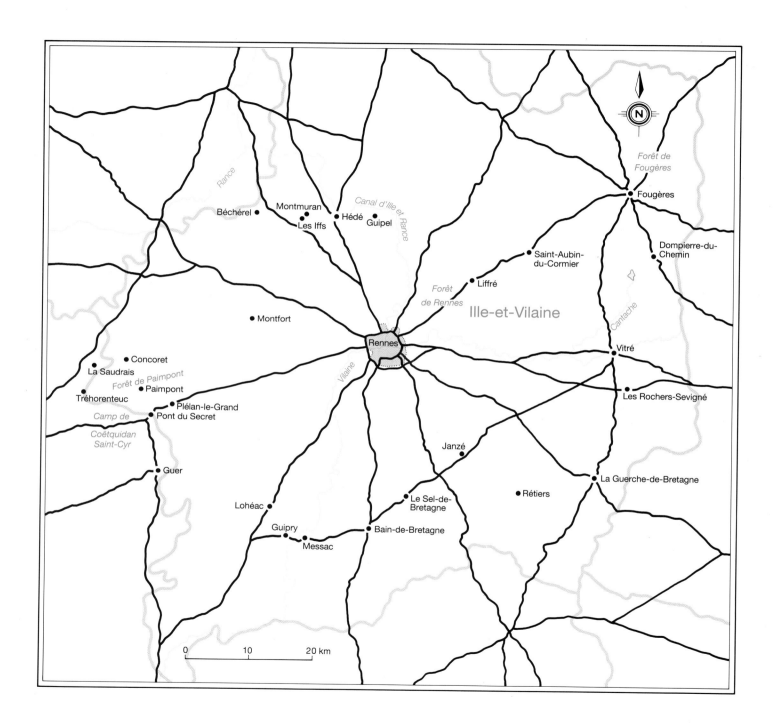

Rance

Canal d'Ille et Rance

Forêt de
Fougères

Béchérel •    • Montmuran      Fougères •
        Les Iffs • • Hédé
                    • Guipel                    Dompierre-du-
                                                Chemin •

                              • Saint-Aubin-
                              du-Cormier

                    Forêt        • Liffré
                    de Rennes
                                        Ille-et-Vilaine            Cantache
    • Montfort

                        Rennes                              Vitré •

    • Concoret
                                                        Les Rochers-Sevigné •
• La Saudrais                Vilaine
    Forêt de Paimpont
• Tréhorenteuc  • Paimpont
                • Plélan-le-Grand
Camp de        • Pont du Secret
                                    • Janzé
Coëtquidan
Saint-Cyr
                                                        • La Guerche-de-Bretagne
    • Guer

            • Lohéac                    • Le Sel-de-        • Rétiers
        Guipry •                        Bretagne
                • Messac    • Bain-de-Bretagne

0        10        20 km

# 6
# The Normandy Borders

*Vitré – Bain-de-Bretagne – Forêt de Paimpont – Montfort*
*Rennes – Fougères*

My copy of Baedeker's *Northern France*, now almost a century old, says of Vitré: 'It still retains some portions of its fortifications, a ruined castle, and numerous quaint medieval houses, and is in this respect one of the most interesting towns in France'. Apart from the castle, which is now far from ruined, this description holds good today; yet for some reason the delights of Vitré seem to be very little known. Though its castle is not as grand as those of Josselin or Fougères, and its medieval streets have been less spruced up than those of Dinan or Vannes, it has its own quiet charm, made up of an intimate unity of ancient buildings, combined with an attractive riverscape where the tranquil waters of the Vilaine bring the countryside right into the heart of the town.

Vitré developed in the Middle Ages as a frontier town, outside the walls of a primitive eleventh-century castle built on a rocky spur of land above the river; the present majestic fortress, with its lofty curtain wall and pointed turrets, dates mainly from the fifteenth century. During the religious wars at the end of the sixteenth century it became a centre for the Protestant Huguenots; and in the following century the Breton parliament (Etats) met there on occasion.

One of their periodic assemblies was attended by Mme de Sévigné, whose gossipy letters give an unrivalled picture of life during the reign of Louis XIV. She lived at the château of Les Rochers outside Vitré, and also had a house in the town. Together with her friend Mme de Chaulnes, wife of the Governor of Brittany, she sat through endless boring provincial festivities, commenting disapprovingly on the opening feast of the Etats of 1671: 'The good cheer was excessive; the roast joints were removed as though they had not been touched; and as for the pyramids of fruit, the doors should have been made higher to let them through.' But all this ostentation was punished: the pyramid of twenty porcelain dishes crashed to the ground, drowning the music of violins and trumpets.

Vitré's castle is still the town's focal point. Its powerful grey walls, chequered with brown ironstone, are built to an unusual triangular plan, dictated by the irregular shape of the site, and it is far more compact and cramped than the conventional square or rectangular castle. A good deal of its limited area is taken up by the pseudo-gothic town hall, built inside the walls in the early years of this century. This means that about half the castle cannot be visited; but it also has

the virtue of bringing the everyday functional life of the town within its walls.

Several of the towers have been turned into small museums. The largest of them, the Tour Saint-Laurent, is full of relics of the old town, among them a section of a magnificent gothic oak staircase, and a series of meticulous watercolour drawings done in 1870 for a nineteenth-century restoration programme – proof that conservation, at least in France, has a far longer pedigree than is generally imagined. At that period Vitré certainly needed preserving, as the Paris-Brest railway had recently cut a brutal swathe through the southern half of the medieval town. The collection in the Tour de l'Argenterie, called the Cabinet des Curiosités, is a typical nineteenth-century hotchpotch ranging from cases of beetles, neatly laid out and labelled, to hideous tableaux of stuffed frogs fencing, dancing and engaged in other unfroglike activities. The dainty renaissance Tour de l'Oratoire, once the castle's private chapel, has some good sixteenth-century Limoges enamels, and various valuable religious objects. As you walk round the walls between the towers, you can look down on gardens butting right up to the castle, where children play while their parents dig up vegetables.

Vitré's main church, the Eglise Notre Dame, is a spectacularly gabled building, built in the fifteenth century in Flamboyant gothic style. The south side has no fewer than seven gables, and a stone open-air pulpit, delicately carved and pinnacled, against one of the buttresses. On the west front is a strange renaissance-style porch, making an incongruous contrast with the gothic façade surrounding it.

Between the château and Notre Dame are the medieval streets, mainly pedestrianized; unusually regular and almost grid-like in their ground plan, they juxtapose every variety of half-timbering, tile-hanging and general decorative effect. The Rue d'En Bas

*The drawbridge and turrets of the Château de Vitré, one of the powerful castles built during the Middle Ages along the borders of Brittany and Normandy.*

*The castle and old town of Vitré seen from the fields outside the town. The River Vilaine runs along the valley below.*

(literally Street from Below, as it leads up steeply from the lower level) has some of the finest of them, notably the Hôtel du Bol d'Or (a private house, not a hotel), with crazy turrets and overhangs added haphazardly down the centuries. The street's continuation, the Rue Poterie, has further fine old buildings, as does the Rue Baudrairie, which leads off it at right-angles. Mme

*A delicately carved and pinnacled stone pulpit built for open-air instruction against the south wall of Vitré's Notre-Dame church.*

de Sévigné has a street named after her at the top end of the Rue Poterie.

Continuing past the south side of the church, turn left down the Promenade du Val, and walk below the battered town wall towards the Vilaine. The promenade continues below the north side of the ramparts, past a medieval postern gate and finally below the curtain wall of the castle, giving wide views over the trees and gardens of the Vilaine valley. Across the river is the medieval monastery of Saint-Nicolas, which functions as a hostel for people disadvantaged in various ways, and employs them in its workshops and garden. Its gothic chapel is now a small museum, centring on a fine effigy tomb of about 1500, which was carved for an almoner of the monastery.

Drive south from Vitré along the D88 to Les Rochers-

Sévigné, Mme de Sévigné's rustic retreat. You would hardly call Les Rochers beautiful, but it is full of character, and consists of three buildings all utterly individual: the fifteenth-century château, with plenty of sharply-pointed turrets, which she inherited; a detached octagonal chapel, which she built in the 1670s; and a fine classical stable block, which dates from the following century. Les Rochers has moved with the times: the stable block is now a golf clubhouse, lined with pictures of famous British golfcourses; while the park that was Mme de Sévigné's pride and joy has been largely turned into the fairways, greens and bunkers of a full-scale eighteen-hole course. Not much of the château is open: only the chapel, decorated in grey, blue and gold; and the workroom, where Mme de Sévigné wrote endless letters looking out over the garden.

The formal gardens leading to the château still have their rows of pleached limes, presumably the descendants of those planted by Mme de Sévigné. She was a great tree-lover, and described her plantings in a letter to her daughter: 'I find these woods of an extraordinary beauty and sadness: all these trees that you have seen so small have become tall, straight and in the perfection of beauty; they have been pruned and give a delightful shade.' Elsewhere she paints a charmingly breathless picture of being caught in a summer downpour, while walking in the woods with her friend Mme de Chaulnes. 'The leaves were saturated one moment, and our clothes were saturated the next. We started to run; we shouted, we fell, we slipped, at last we got home, we lit a great fire; we changed our blouses and skirts . . . we split our sides laughing.'

Drive south on the D178 to La Guerche-de-Bretagne, a small country town with a central square of fine old houses, and a thirteenth-century church enlarged and rebuilt at various periods. The most curious thing

*In the small country town of La Guerche-de-Bretagne, an elaborately half-timbered medieval house overlooks the main square.*

about La Guerche is its name, which is said to derive from the Frankish word *werki*, meaning a fortified hill (G replacing W, as in William and Guillaume).

From La Guerche, head west along the D47 to Rétiers, where signposts point you in the direction of La Roche-aux-Fées, one of the most important megalithic monuments in the whole of France. Some time around 3000 BC over forty giant blocks were hauled into place to form an *allée couverte* or passage grave; made of red schist, they had to be manhandled 4 kilometres cross-country from their place of origin. The locals used to say that it was impossible to count them exactly, as the fairies who built the passage and gave their name to it were in league with the Devil, who was a master of deceit. Before a couple got married, the man would walk clockwise round the stones while the woman went anti-clockwise, both counting as they went. If they came up with the same number, the wedding went ahead; but if their numbers were different, they called it off.

Make for Janzé, which has an unusually large church, then follow the D777 through Le Sel-de-Bretagne, once a salt-trading centre, to Bain-de-Bretagne. This small crossroads town, on the main road between Rennes and Nantes, used to be choked with traffic, but has recently been transformed by a new bypass, combined with a labyrinthine one-way system. It is worth stopping for a stroll down to the peaceful little lake on the south side of the town. A short way to the west, beside the D772, the austere seventeenth-century chapel of Notre Dame du Coudray stands in a grove of trees. A stone in the transept has a cavity the size and shape of a child's foot; in the old days, mothers of children with walking problems used to put their feet into the cavity in the hope of a miraculous cure.

The statue of the Virgin kept in the chapel is said to have been found in the sixteenth century, after a child was miraculously rescued from drowning in a nearby pond. As its mother watched helplessly, a pair of mysterious hands dragged it from the water and laid it down on the bank. When the pond was drained, the statue was discovered in the mud, and the chapel was built to house it. Our Lady of Le Coudray is credited with the salvation of Bain-de-Bretagne towards the end of World War II. In August 1944 the Germans were on the point of burning the town and shooting twelve hostages, including the mayor and the *curé*, in reprisal for troops killed by the Resistance. While the congregation was praying to the Virgin for deliverance, Allied aircraft appeared providentially in the sky, a convoy of American tanks rolled into the town, and Bain-de-Bretagne was saved.

Drive south down the N137, then fork right on the D57 to the small town of Le Grand Fougeray. On its southern edge is a tall fourteenth-century *donjon* or keep – all that survives of one of the major strongholds of the Hundred Years War. In 1356 it was captured from the English by Du Guesclin, in one of his most daring exploits. Disguised as a woodcutter, he talked his way into the castle accompanied by 30 soldiers carrying firewood. Once inside, they threw down their bundles, drew their swords and butchered the garrison.

Head north-west up the D69 to Messac, which shares a joint waterfront with the village of Guipry, on the opposite side of the Vilaine. From the canal basin, cruising boats of every shape and size can sail north up the Vilaine to Rennes and link up with Canal d'Ille et Rance, navigable right up to Dinan and Saint-Malo; or they can head south to join the Nantes-Brest Canal at Redon.

Beyond Guipry, take the D772 by way of Lohéac to Guer, and then turn north along the D773. This takes you past the officer-training centre of Coëtquidan Saint-Cyr, on the edge of a huge plateau of heathland largely given over to military manoeuvres. Beyond the roadside barrack blocks, make for the little town of Paimpont, at the centre of the forest to which it has given its name, and legendary heart of the part of Brittany most closely linked with folk-memories of

*The grim keep of Le Grand Fougeray, all that survives of a medieval fortress that once had a curtain wall with nine towers.*

King Arthur, his knights, and all the wizards, magicians, fairies and damsels associated with him.

Paimpont itself is an unusual and attractive little town, with a single main street which is reached through an ancient gate, and leads to an abbey founded in the seventh century. The present church, large and barn-like, with a squat central tower, was built in the thirteenth century and has been much altered since. A wing of the monastic buildings is now used as the town hall. Behind the abbey paths radiate from a peaceful lake into the surrounding woodland.

The Forêt de Paimpont is all that survives of the vast Brocéliande forest which once extended over much of central Brittany. There is no point in trying to work out any circuit of the forest; rather, you should just drive, or preferably walk, through its alternations of overshadowing trees and open glades, in the certainty of getting lost sooner or later, as happens in all proper forests. A good place to begin your exploration is at the Château de Comper, about 6 kilometres north of Paimpont. A few massive walls survive from the medieval castle, reached across a dry moat, where a sign bears the unlikely warning *Danger – Vipères*. Today's château is a nineteenth-century gabled farm-house, which has clearly seen better days. Most of it is closed, though a couple of large rooms on the ground floor are used in summer for exhibitions devoted to Arthurian themes.

Local enthusiasts hope to turn Comper into some kind of Arthurian centre, due mainly to its position at the head of a broad lake steeped in legend. This was the water from which Sir Lancelot took the name Lancelot du Lac; and somewhere beneath its surface the enchantress Viviane had her underwater palace. When I first saw the lake in the 1970s it filled its basin right up to the surrounding trees and lapped against the embankment below the château; but in 1990, after

*The stone-edged basin of the Fontaine de Barenton, said to have been a centre of Druid healing, in the heart of the Forêt de Paimpont. The forest also has legendary connections with King Arthur.*

successive summer droughts, it had shrunk to about half its former size. If it ever dries out entirely, who knows what fragments of knightly armour, or bones of heroes lured to their doom, may be found embedded in its mud?

Viviane also haunts the remote Fontaine de Barenton, on the other side of Paimpont from Comper. Hidden high among the trees, Barenton lies twenty minutes up a track from a small car-park near the village of La Saudrais. The woodland is a good deal more open than it used to be, as about half the big trees were destroyed in the hurricane of October 1987, but it still has the magical feeling of a forest that has remained inviolate since prehistoric times. It was here that Viviane fell in love with Merlin and imprisoned him within a magic circle she drew around the fountain.

The Druids have also been linked with Barenton, which was a centre of their teaching. Certainly there are enough oak trees in the neighbourhood to make this probable (the name 'Druid' derives from the Greek *drus*, meaning an oak), and the coffin-shaped stone basin of the spring would have been just the right size for some kind of total-immersion ritual. The water, which is at a constant temperature of 10 °C and is rich in carbonic acid, is said to be good for the treatment of rickets and mental disorders, and was no doubt used by the Druids for their cures. Perhaps the name of the hamlet down below, Folle-Pensée ('Mad Thought'), enshrines some water-based healing régime practised in these woods 2000 years ago.

Druid tradition and Arthurian legend meet at Barenton in a stone beside the spring called the Perron de Merlin ('Merlin's Threshold'). Merlin is said to have suffered from a nervous disorder and to have been treated at the Druids' clinic; and it was while he was sleeping by the fountain that Viviane got him into her power. In past centuries a silver cup was attached to the stone by a chain, and if a passer-by scooped up a cupful of water and sprinkled it on the stone, there would immediately be a downpour of rain, followed by a flock of sweetly singing birds. The efficacy of this ritual was believed in throughout the Middle Ages; a fifteenth-century writer tells us that whenever the

175

lord of Montfort visited Barenton and tipped water on the stone, 'no matter how hot it was, it rained abundantly on the land'. Four centuries later Hersart de la Villemarqué described the same ritual carried out by the priest of Concoret village, 'in procession headed by crucifix and banners, singing hymns and ringing bells'. But alas, by this time the world had grown more cynical, and, says Hersart, 'no one told me whether he succeeded in gathering the storm clouds together'.

From Barenton, make for the little church at Tréhorenteuc, down the hill a few kilometres away. With its broach spire it looks as though it has strayed into Brittany from southern England. Inside it is a riot of paintings and stained glass, mostly fairly recent and on the lurid side, showing Arthur, his knights, the Round Table, the Holy Grail, Excalibur and all the rest of the Arthurian pantheon. The local saint, St Omenne, who gave away all her goods and became a nun, has her place too in the decorative scheme, but is inevitably put in the shade by so much mock-medievalism.

Tréhorenteuc is the starting-point for a short walk round the Val Sans Retour ('Valley of No Return'). It was once the home of King Arthur's evil sister, Morgana, who would lure her lovers there and keep them under a spell. Thus she ensured that they stayed faithful to her for ever, as they could never leave the valley. When I last went there, there had just been a forest fire and the hillside was covered with the blackened skeletons of pine trees and gorse. But the deciduous trees round the lake in the bottom of the valley had somehow survived, the green of their leaves making a brilliant contrast with the wilderness all around; perhaps the flames had jumped the valley.

Nearby is the Forêt de Paimpont's only real castle, the Château de Trécesson, a pretty fifteenth-century miniature fortress reflected in its moat. It can only be seen from the outside, as it is strictly *propriété privée*. Not far from Trécesson I drove up a track for a picnic lunch and found a forgotten country chapel, still in use though battered-looking, with tumbledown byres and a farmhouse attached: typical of the unknown treasures that can still be discovered a hundred metres from the road throughout Brittany.

Back on the main road (N24), head towards Rennes by way of a riverside hamlet called the Pont du Secret, where Queen Guinevere confessed her love to Sir Lancelot. Past Plélan-le-Grand, fork left on the D61 for Montfort, a small fortified town high above the River Meu. A castle was built here about 1100, destroyed in the twelfth century, and rebuilt towards the end of the fourteenth; its huge keep, made of local red and green stone, dominates the town centre.

For centuries Montfort was known as 'Montfort-la-Cane' ('Montfort the Duck'), after a legendary event said to have taken place in 1386. A beautiful girl from a nearby village came to the castle one day, bringing food to her father who was working on the fortifications. She took the fancy of the lecherous lord of Montfort, who locked her up in a tower when she refused his advances. Calling on St Nicholas, patron saint of virgins in distress, she was at once transformed into a duck and flew from the tower, leaving her webbed footprints on the windowsill. For several centuries afterwards a duck, with a dozen ducklings strung out behind her, regularly attended Mass in Montfort church on the anniversary of the miracle.

From Montfort, take the D72 north to Bécherel another small fortified town, which still has part of its medieval ramparts and a few fine old houses. In feudal times the lord of Bécherel had an unusual (and unusually pointless) right over his vassals: on Easter Monday he would burn any hemp or flax that had not been got ready for weaving, to teach the townswomen not to be lazy.

Just west of the village is the eighteenth-century Château de Caradeuc. Nicknamed the 'Versailles of Brittany' because of the classical symmetry of its design – though it is far from Versailles-like in scale – it

*The fifteenth-century Château de Trécesson, on the outskirts of the Forêt de Paimpont, reflected in its moat. Near by is the so-called 'Valley of No Return', where Arthur's evil sister Morgana is said to have imprisoned her lovers.*

lies on a north-facing ridge, overlooking a wide panorama across the Rance valley. It was built in the 1720s by the Breton politician Anne-Nicolas de Caradeuc, and belonged to the fervent eighteenth-century Breton nationalist Le Chalotais, who opposed the authority of central government from Paris and was imprisoned for his beliefs. The château is surrounded by the largest formal park in Brittany, laid out with broad grassy walks, and filled with statues of mythological and historical figures. It lost many of its magnificent trees in the hurricane of October 1987, but a replanting programme is now well under way. (The park is open to the public, but the château is not.)

East of Bécherel, on the other side of the main road (D27), the small parish of Les Iffs is unusual in having both a splendid church and a noble château within its boundaries. Its name means 'The Yews', and refers to the trees planted in the graveyard. The church is one of the finest in the region, and was built in the fourteenth and fifteenth centuries in Flamboyant gothic style by the Laval family, lords of the town of Tinténiac, who lived at Montmuran near by. The large west porch was built so that lepers could take part in the mass without entering the church. The superb stained-glass windows, Breton-made but inspired by Flemish originals, illustrate such themes as Susannah and the Elders, the beheading of John the Baptist and the Last Judgment, in colours which have kept their glowing intensity for more than four centuries.

Montmuran château, stronghold of the Lavals, was built in stages from the twelfth to the eighteenth century, and stands on a rocky promontory at the end of a long avenue of oak and beech. Its imposing medieval gatehouse still has a drawbridge in working order. Bertrand du Guesclin was knighted in the chapel in 1354, and married his second wife, Jeanne de Laval, there in 1373. One of Montmuran's fireplaces has a unique back-boiler water-heating system behind

*Glowing sixteenth-century stained glass in the chapel of Les Iffs, near Bécherel. Breton-made, it was inspired by Flemish work.*

the hearth, which has been variously dated to the Middle Ages and the eighteenth century.

In Brittany, all roads lead to Rennes, and from Les Iffs the most direct route is along the N137. But a far more enjoyable, and peaceful, way of getting there is via the pretty hilltop town of Hédé, which has a fine twelfth-century romanesque church, the ruins of a medieval keep, and a spectacular flight of eleven stepwise locks ('Les Onze Ecluses') on the Ille et Rance canal. From Hédé, make for the village of Guipel, then turn south down the D82 for Rennes.

The capital city both of Brittany as a whole and of the Département d'Ille-et-Vilaine, Rennes breathes an air of solid prosperity. Across its centre runs the Vilaine, which has been tamed by high stone embankments, or driven underground by the need to provide more parking space. On either side the *quais* are lined

*The dignified terrace staircase of the eighteenth-century Château de Caradeuc, which has been nicknamed the 'Versailles of Brittany'. It is set in a fine park.*

*A painted wooden carving of a peasant on a house in the Rue de la Psalette, Rennes. The street gets its name from the room where the cathedral choir practised their psalm-singing.*

by respectable classical buildings. The Vilaine runs due east–west; the north–south axis, equally regular, intersects it at the flowery parterres in front of the Palais du Commerce. Rennes has one of the finest botanic gardens in France, the Jardin du Thabor and its associated Jardin des Plantes; and every open space is ablaze with meticulously laid-out flowerbeds, the plantings changing as the year progresses.

Rennes (Roazon in Breton) takes its name from the Redones, one of the Celtic tribes of pre-Roman times, whose name survives unaltered in the nearby town of Redon. By the third century AD it was a strongly fortified town, built at the strategic point where the Ille joins the Vilaine, and standing at the junction of three major Roman roads. Not much is known about Rennes under the Romans, apart from the fact that it

probably covered the same area as the medieval town, around the cathedral. At the time of the decay of the Roman Empire in the fifth century it was the seat of a bishopric, and was known as the *Urbs Rubra*, the 'Rose-red City', from the pink courses of Roman brick in the stone wall surrounding it.

Begin your exploration of Rennes in this ancient part. The cathedral, dedicated to St Peter, is a dull building, with a ponderous baroque façade built between 1540 and 1700, and a mid nineteenth-century interior, all gilding and elephantine polished columns; its main treasure is a sixteenth-century Flemish altarpiece, illustrating scenes from the life of the Virgin. Near by is the Porte Mordelaise, a fortified gateway through which the dukes of Brittany used to pass in solemn procession to be crowned in the cathedral; and round it are a few cramped streets lined with medieval houses, among them the Rue de la Monnaie, once the site of the city's mint, and the Rue de la Psalette, so called from the room where the cathedral choir practised their psalm-singing. The Place des Lices ('Square of the Lists', or 'Tiltyard'), recently extensively restored, recalls the days when Bertrand du Guesclin and his fellow knights charged each other in the tournament.

You will look in vain in Rennes for the extensive medieval quarters to be found in towns such as Vannes or Quimper. This is because in 1720 most of the ancient centre east of the cathedral was destroyed in a disastrous fire, started one December night by a drunken workman who set light to his lodgings. Well over 900 buildings were burnt down; but the Rennais took advantage of the destruction to lay out a brand-new grid pattern of houses built to a standardized design, consisting of cellar, arcaded ground floor for shops and craftsmen, three accommodation storeys and an attic. The original severity of the design was overlaid down the years by a rash of shop fascias, but

*An unusually large expanse of half-timbering in the Place des Lices, the medieval heart of Rennes. Much of the old city was burned down in 1720.*

most of these have now been removed, leaving the arcading restored to its original simplicity.

The grandest of the buildings to escape the fire was the Palais de Justice, once the seat of the Breton Parliament (Etats). Completed by about 1655, its dignified façade, two storeys high and with a tall mansard roof, was designed by Salomon de Brosse (1571–1626), architect of the Palais de Luxembourg in Paris. The most spectacular of the rooms on view is the Grande Chambre du Parlement de Bretagne, richly painted and gilded, and hung with tapestries. The two loggias jutting from the walls were for ladies to follow the course of the Etats' debates; the smaller of the two was much used by Mme de Sévigné, who described the Palais de Justice as *le plus beau de France*.

A little way south of the Palais, towards the river, is the Eglise Saint-Germain, which marks the eastern limit of the 1720 conflagration and is the best of Rennes' old churches. It dates from about 1500 and is an odd-shaped building, with a noble interior and fine east window. Over the altar is a spectacular baldacchino, white-painted and gilded. Up the hill from the river is the big church of Saint-Melaine, all that is left of the Benedictine monastery that once stood there. It conceals a medieval interior behind a baroque façade, and is worth a look inside for the fifteenth-century fresco in the south transept.

Behind Saint-Melaine the monastic garden is now the Jardin du Thabor, which stands on the highest plateau in Rennes and was probably named by the monks after the biblical Mount Tabor. Laid out mainly in the second half of the nineteenth century, it shows the French art of formal gardening to perfection, with flowerbeds tightly planted in abstract patterns, in animal outlines, or in the pattern of Brittany's coat of arms. Here you can stroll on the lawns under magnificent specimen trees, buy a drink in the glass-roofed orangery, or explore the enormous rose garden, where hundreds of labelled varieties are arranged in concentric circles, separated by paths. You can even play ping-pong on a weather-proof, and vandal-proof, outdoor table, made of stone with a metal net.

Not far away, in the Rue Hoche, I found a bakery selling more than thirty kinds of bread, among them 'Berlin bread' to eat with chicken, cumin bread to go with strong cheese, chocolate bread, onion bread, aniseed bread, and *pain biologique*, which sounds like a healthy diet carried to extremes. The proprietor, Monsieur Cozic, 'researches ancient methods of manufacture and different recipes in danger of disappearing', and his bread certainly makes a change from *baguettes* morning, noon and night.

Walking down from the Thabor along the Rue Gambetta, you pass the most immediately striking of all the buildings in Rennes – the Palais Saint-Georges, a massive arcaded palace built as a convent for Benedictine nuns in 1650, and still bearing the name 'Magdelaine de Lafayette' (the abbess who commissioned the convent) in huge letters above the arcading.

Everything so far described is on the north side of the Vilaine, which is the most interesting part of Rennes to explore on foot. However, the city's main museum is across the river, on the Quai Emile Zola, in a sober stone mid nineteenth-century building. It is in fact two museums in one: the Beaux-Arts, on the first floor, with plenty of Dutch and Italian paintings; and the Musée de Bretagne, on the ground floor, which is in itself a potted history of the country.

As you would expect, the Beaux-Arts has a good many paintings by Breton artists. A monumental canvas by Charles Cottet, painted in 1903, shows a group of coiffed women from Plougastel sitting down to a picnic on the grass, while the *pardon* of St Anne-la-Palud goes on round the chapel behind them. There are also several paintings of harbour and street scenes by Jean-Julien Lemordant, who was born in Saint-Malo in 1878 and was active in the early years of this century. As well as its pictures, the Beaux-Arts has a fine collection of pottery from Rennes, Quimper and Dinan.

In the Musée de Bretagne you can learn about the geology of Brittany, pore over documents dealing with

*The Jardin du Thabor in Rennes, the finest example of French formal gardening in a city justly famous for its public gardens.*

episodes of Breton history, look at traditional box-beds, chests and other furniture, or study cases of costumes ranging from the puritan-looking clothes of Saint-Malo to the cheerful garments from Cornouaille. A modern audio-visual section covers events and trends in Brittany over the past few decades, among them rural depopulation and unemployment, the impact of tourism on the region, and the revival of a sense of Breton identity.

As far as Rennes itself is concerned, the event of greatest historical significance was the Révolte du Papier Timbré, which took place in 1675. It got its name from the stamped paper on which official documents were written, devised as a means of raising money by Colbert, Louis XIV's finance minister. Not only was there a tax on stamped paper, but taxes were imposed on tobacco and pewter ware as well. The revolt began outside Brittany, in Bordeaux, in March 1675; and in April the inhabitants of Rennes followed suit. The centre for tobacco distribution was sacked, as were the offices concerned with stamped paper and excise dues.

The Duc de Chaulnes, governor of Brittany and friend of Mme de Sévigné, was given the task of putting down the rebellion, which by midsummer had spread over most of Brittany and was taking on the dimensions of a full-scale revolution. Organized bands of peasants, known as Bonnets Rouges from their distinctive headgear, were scouring the countryside urging their fellows to throw off not only their tax burdens, but also the feudal fetters of statute labour carried out for their overlords, and the tithes levied to support the parish priests.

The rebellion ended as suddenly as it began, when Sébastien Le Balp, its only competent leader, was killed and his supporters dispersed. The Duc de Chaulnes took terrible reprisals on the peasants, hanging them by the dozen without trial. After suppressing the countryside he turned his attention to Rennes, where he razed one of the most prosperous suburbs to the ground and exiled the Etats to Vannes. The ringleaders of the revolt were hanged or broken on the wheel, and 10,000 troops were posted to Brittany for the winter,

where they behaved like an army of occupation, looting and raping, and throwing householders from their windows. Early in 1676 an amnesty was declared, and Brittany slowly returned to normal. In retrospect, the Révolte du Papier Timbré seems like a rehearsal for the Revolution which was to take place a century later.

Around the historic centre, modern Rennes sprawls for a couple of kilometres out to its *rocade* (ring road), and has begun to leapfrog over it in places. With its university complex, one of the world's most up-to-date centres of electronic teaching, on the north-east side of the city, its space-age tower blocks, its sports complexes and booming industry, it is the only city in Brittany that can be compared with France's other great provincial centres such as Lyon or Tours. (I leave Nantes out of the reckoning, as it is no longer officially in Brittany.) Yet in spite of its cosmopolitan air, Rennes is still wholeheartedly Breton: witness its annual July celebration, the Tombées de la Nuit ('Nightfalls'), a week-long street festival largely devoted to Breton performing arts.

Leaving Rennes, head through the north-eastern suburbs on the Fougères road (N12), which slices as straight as a die through the noble trees of the Forêt de Rennes, one of the city's main country lungs. Fortunately you can soon forget the headlong traffic by taking one of the network of minor roads that crisscross the forest. Apart from the area round Paimpont, this remains about the most heavily wooded part of Brittany, with further extensive stretches round Liffré and Saint-Aubin-du-Cormier.

Saint-Aubin is famous in Breton history as the place where Brittany's independence received its death-blow, though it kept a vestige of autonomy up to its full union with France in 1532. In 1488 the French army, under Charles VIII, invaded Brittany after the Breton Duke François II had allied himself with the English; and on July 28 that year a motley force made

*The town of Saint-Aubin-du-Cormier is dominated by a huge basilica, built about 1900, though it looks genuinely romanesque.*

up of the Bretons and their allies was routed by the French on heathland north of Saint-Aubin. The site of the battle is marked by a granite memorial beside the D794, a kilometre north of the N12. Erected to mark the 500th anniversary of the battle, it commemorates all those who died 'for the independence and honour of Brittany', listing them as 6000 Bretons, 3500 Gascons, Basques and Spaniards, 800 soldiers of the Holy Roman Emperor, and 500 English archers – an indication of the numbers and nationalities of the mercenaries who sold their services in war-torn fifteenth-century Europe.

The little town of Saint-Aubin is on the other side of the main road, dominated by a large grey basilica which at first sight looks romanesque but in fact dates from around 1900. Saint-Aubin's ruined medieval castle lies behind the church; built commandingly on a rocky spur above the Couesnon, its past magnificence is recalled by the remains of its walls, a tall round tower that rises sheer for 30m or so, and a rose window in what is left of the chapel. The castle had the briefest of lives: completed only in 1486, it was destroyed two years later on the orders of Charles VIII.

In contrast with the shattered ruins of the château of Saint-Aubin, the castle of Fougères, 20 kilometres up the road, is the epitome of feudal military grandeur. In summer, multi-coloured pennons flutter from its pointed turrets; and its strong walls, now with gardens, cafés and car-parks at their foot, still look capable of keeping invading armies at bay, as they did for centuries. The plan of the castle is mainly due to Baron Raoul II of Fougères, who rebuilt it in 1173 after it had been destroyed in the previous decade by Henry II of England. The ring of towers that are its chief glory, among them the poetically named Tour Raoul, Tour Surienne, Tour Mélusine and Tour du Gobelin, date mainly from the fourteenth and fifteenth cen-

*The turreted curtain wall of the castle of Fougères, which rivals Vitré in grandeur. Its ring of defensive towers epitomizes the military architecture of the Middle Ages.*

turies. The site seems oddly chosen, down in a valley and dominated from the high ground where the main town of Fougères now stands; but the rock outcrop on which the castle is built was originally surrounded entirely by a loop of the River Nançon, except for a narrow neck of land at the main entrance.

Apart from the scale of its walls and towers, which alone make it worth a visit, the château has all sorts of fascinating details. By the entrance there is a group of four overshot water-wheels, which once provided power for grinding the garrison's corn. Once inside the castle, look out for the Tour Coigny, a fortified tower turned into a chapel in the seventeenth century. The Tour Raoul, one of the grandest of them all, contains a small footwear museum (open irregularly), with shoes of every conceivable foot-distorting shape from the seventeenth century on – a collection of particular relevance to Fougères, as the town has been a centre of shoe manufacture since the 1860s.

The lower town (Ville Basse) across the castle moat is a good place to wander about in, with its half-timbered houses and the fine old church of Saint-Sulpice. Built in the fifteenth century in Flamboyant gothic style, it has an unusually tall and slender tower and spire covered in slates, with a needle-sharp spirelet at each corner. The gargoyles at roof level are exceptionally large and menacing. Inside is a miracle-working statue of the Virgin suckling the infant Jesus, which was recovered from the castle moat in the fourteenth century after being thrown there 200 years earlier by the English. A small granite carving above the door on the south side of the church shows the fairy Mélusine – legendary protectress of the Lusignan family, who were the lords of Fougères in the years round 1300 – combing her hair in a mirror.

A seventeenth-century chaplain of Saint-Sulpice, the Abbé Poussinière, was famous in his day for such magical feats as offering his friends fresh cherries from his cherry tree on Christmas Day, and causing a shower of ink to fall on some girls who were parading round Fougères in dresses too low-cut for his taste. He also flew through the air 'as swiftly as an arrow' from Fougères to Rennes in five minutes instead of the usual four and a half hours. However, his supernatural powers, real or imagined, did not endear him to the church authorities, and in 1642 he was burnt at the stake in Rennes.

From the castle and lower town, steep streets climb to the upper town (Ville Haute) where today Fougères goes about its business. The fine public gardens up here give exceptional views, northwards over the castle and lower town to a backcloth of cliffs, and south-west towards Rennes, across a seemingly endless tree-covered plain. The church of Saint-Léonard, which forms one side of the garden, has gargoyles as imposing as those of Saint-Sulpice.

Though it seems modern in comparison with the lower town, the upper town was also in existence in medieval times. Much of it was accidentally burnt down in 1710, as happened in Rennes at much the same period, and the houses were rebuilt on an eighteenth-century grid layout, in granite instead of inflammable half-timbering. The main streets of the rebuilding are the parallel Rue Nationale and Rue Chateaubriand, lined with sober stone houses, apart from a single timber-framed survivor of the fire supported on pillars over the pavement.

Fougères' street-corner signs have a nice touch: they include a potted history of the street in question. Thus the sign in the Place du Théâtre tells you that it stands on the site of the ancient salt-trading quarter, and was the first open square to be laid out in a close-packed medieval town. Just off the Rue Nationale is the upper town's chief architectural curiosity – a detached octagonal belfry dating from the fourteenth century.

During the Revolution Fougères had its share of troubles, as it was a centre of the Chouan pro-Royalist movement. The Marquis de la Rouërie, one of the first heroes of Chouannerie, was born in the town in 1750, and in 1788 was sent by the Etats to plead the rights of the Bretons before Louis XVI. The king threw him briefly into the Bastille for his pains, but in spite of such treatment La Rouërie reckoned that the *ancien régime* was better than anything the Revolution could offer. He founded his own anti-Revolutionary movement, the Association Bretonne, which planned a full-scale uprising. But in 1793, before the uprising could take place, La Rouërie learnt that the king had been guillotined; already suffering from exhaustion, he died of shock when he heard the news.

Just north of the town, the Forêt de Fougères was a refuge for the Chouans; the Croix de Récouvrance, on its northern edge, was one of their early rallying-places. As you walk along the forest paths below magnificent beech trees, you come across all sorts of megaliths and unexplained workings, above and below ground. Most mysterious of them are the huge vaulted cellars known as the Celliers de Landéan, which are said to have been dug in the twelfth century by Raoul II, builder of Fougères castle, to keep his treasures safe from the English. You reach them down a flight of stone steps, but they are kept locked, and you can only get an idea of their size by flashing a torch between the bars of an iron grille.

From Fougères you can return to Vitré direct along the D178; or, for a final dip into the limitless well of Breton legend, take the D798 to Dompierre-du-Chemin. Just south of the village, near the point where the road crosses the Cantache river, a track leads up to rocky bluffs facing each other across a ravine. This is the site of the Saut Roland ('Roland's Leap'), where the great Paladin, returning from Spain to his domains in Brittany after fighting the Saracens, chanced his luck once too often. Rather than find an easier but longer route, Roland prayed to God to help him, spurred his horse and leaped from one side of the ravine to the other. Full of bravado, he appealed to the Virgin and managed the return leap; but the third time, when he called on the name of his lady-love, the exhausted horse missed its footing and fell into the ravine, taking the hero to his death. Down-to-earth chroniclers tell us that Roland was killed in battle at Roncesvalles – but the Bretons, as always, have a better story.

---

*The site of the Saut Roland ('Roland's Leap'), near Dompierre-du-Chemin, where Charlemagne's famous warrior is said to have plunged to his death, still mounted on his horse.*

# Index